The Rise of Islam

This Volume is dedicated to

Peter Avery

The Rise of Islam

The Idea of Iran

Volume IV

Edited By

Vesta Sarkhosh Curtis

and

Sarah Stewart

in association with The London Middle East Institute at SOAS
and
The British Museum

Supported by the Soudavar Memorial Foundation

I.B. TAURIS
LONDON · NEW YORK

Published in 2009 by I.B.Tauris & Co Ltd
6 Salem Road, London W2 4BU
175 Fifth Avenue, New York NY 10010
www.ibtauris.com

Distributed in the United States and Canada Exclusively
by Palgrave Macmillan
175 Fifth Avenue, New York NY 10010

ISBN 978 1 84511 691 0

The Idea of Iran Vol. 4

A full CIP record for this book is available from the British Library
A full CIP record is available from the Library of Congress

Library of Congress Catalogue Card Number: available

Typeset by P. Fozooni

Printed and bound in Great Britain by CPI Antony Rowe, Chippenham from camera-ready copy edited and supplied by the editors

Contents

List of Figures

Acknowledgements

The editors are grateful to the Trustees of the Soudavar Memorial Foundation for sponsoring the symposia and making the publication of the proceedings possible. In particular, we are indebted to Mrs Fatema Soudavar-Farmanfarmaian for her help, advice and involvement in the planning of each symposium.

This volume would not have been possible without the input and expertise of Dr. Parvis Fozooni, who once again has formatted and typeset this volume with his usual dedication and eye for detail. We are also grateful to Burzine Waghmar for copyediting the papers.

We would like to thank Iradj Bagherzade, Alex Wright and staff at I.B.Tauris for their help in producing the publication.

Finally, our thanks go to the authors who submitted their papers, thereby making it possible to publish this series in record time.

Introduction

Vesta Sarkhosh Curtis (The British Museum)

and

Sarah Stewart (The London Middle East Institute at SOAS)

The fourth volume in the series *The Idea of Iran* deals with the transition from pre-Islamic Sasanian Iran, in which Zoroastrianism was the state religion, to the Arab conquest of Iran and subsequent adoption of Islam. This transitional period is of utmost importance to our understanding of the history of Iran and its subsequent development. The seven papers presented in this volume document some of the changes that took place as the new ruling elite established its system of governance.

As in previous volumes in this series, contributions are drawn from different disciplines including history, art, religion, literature and science. In this volume, we have brought together scholars who are well known for their expertise in both Arab and Persian culture and, once again, the question of Iranian identity is of paramount importance here. Each scholar addresses a different aspect of the remarkable survival of 'Iranianness' during this crucial transitional period.

Despite the loss of the old religion, the impact of Islam and the ethnicity of the new rulers, it was at this time that the foundations were laid for the flowering of the New Persian language and the emergence of a new period of Persian culture.

The opening chapter gives an overview of late Sasanian Iran and questions the reasons for the collapse of this once mighty empire. Professor Ehsan Yarshater suggests that a major factor contributing to the decline of the Sasanian dynasty was no more than 'old age'. By the end of the reign of Khusrau II, the Sasanian empire was in decline. It was at this time that the Arabs of *Hejaz,* driven by their new religion, were empowered to sweep through vast territories of the ancient Near East introducing Islam to the region. Yarshater draws attention to the triumphal element during this period of political defeat, which manifests itself in the uprising in eastern Iran that lead to the downfall of the Ummayad dynasty and the rise of the Abbasid Caliphate. He refers to 'a distinct Iranian identity within the Islamic world' and the 'effervescence of cultural energy in Iran during the early centuries of Islam'.

Hugh Kennedy poses the question of why Iran did not become an Arab country in light of the Islamic conquests of other areas such as Syria, Iraq and Egypt where Arabic became the *lingua franca* replacing Greek, Pahlavi and Aramaic. The administrative legacy of the Sasanian king of kings as well as the continued adherence to Iranian cultural values are two of the reasons put forward by Kennedy to account for the successful preservation of Iranian identity. He also points to the fact that 'Iranian elites adopted and adapted Islam'. Particularly interesting is Kennedy's discussion of the various local Iranian dynasties in northern Iran, such as the Ispahbads of Tabaristan who, partly as a result of their geographic isolation south of the Caspian Sea, were able to retain a level of autonomy in exchange for the payment of tribute to the Muslim authorities. In the south- eastern part of the Caspian, the Bawandids, who converted to Islam in the ninth century, kept their political independence and cultural identity until the Mongol conquests in the fourteenth century. Their continued use of royal names such as Shapur, Shahriyar, Rustam and Dara reflect their ties with pre-Islamic Iran. Other interesting insights include the survival of Persian elites after the Abbasid Revolution of 750 CE (in contrast with the decline of the gentry in Byzantine Egypt) as well as what Kennedy refers to as the 'overtly hereditary nature of status in the Iranian world'. Evidence of this is provided by the bibliographic dictionaries that survive from this period, and appear unique to Iran, as well as the literary narratives of pre-Islamic Iran that came to be incorporated in New Persian literature.

Edmund Bosworth continues with the legacy of Sasanian Iran and the impact it had on local dynasties in the early Islamic period. He also points to 'princely lines' in the Caspian regions, whose genealogies could be traced back to the Sasanians. Like Kennedy, he suggests that the continued links with the past was one of the main reasons why some areas of Iran were able to keep their political independence. Of outstanding importance in the history of tenth century Iran is the emergence of the Buyid dynasty which, by the beginning of the eleventh century had extended control over territories from northern Mesopotamia to southeastern Iran. An important manifestation of the Buyid's 'nostalgia for the ancient Persian past' is the adoption of the royal title king of kings by the Buyid rulers. In eastern Iran the Samanids of Transoxania and Khorasan contributed significantly to the renaissance of a New Persian language and literature – culminating in Firdausi's *Shāhnāma.* By the time this epic was completed, the Ghaznavids had seized power from the Samanids.

Richard Bulliet begins his chapter by asking whether the flourishing of Islamic Iran can be ascribed to the dynamism of the newly arrived conquerors or to the native Iranians. He points to the fact that after the collapse of the Ummayad dynasty, the political fragmentation of Iran has made it difficult to treat its history as a whole. He suggests that we turn to the economic and social spheres in order to understand the narrative of Iran's political history. Bulliet focuses on a particular 'moment' in that development, the astonishing 'boom and bust' that occurred in the economy, which was the result of the introduction of cotton-growing to the Iranian plateau. Not only was this industry lucrative, but it also served to create new urban centres based on the many processes involved in the manufacturing and export of cotton. Particularly interesting is the fact that the use of fabric made from cotton was underpinned by religious precepts. The new religious elite celebrated its importance and simplicity as opposed to fabrics such as silk that had been favoured during the Sasanian period: 'the *'ulema* of the Muslim community, through their endorsement of cotton consumption and deep involvement in its production stood at the centre of urbanisation and commerce'. Signs of economic stress began in the 10th century with the waning of the cotton boom; but it was a major shift in climate, the 'Big Chill' that set in during the 11th century that Bulliet suggests is the main reason for the downturn in the economy that lasted over a century. Although relatively short-lived, this remarkable period of prosperity had a lasting effect on the social, economic, religious, linguistic and political developments both within Iran and far beyond its borders.

Lutz Richter-Bernburg looks at the contributions of Islamic scholars to the field of science and medicine and the way they were viewed by Europeans during the second half the tenth century. Through oranges, quiddities and algorisms he addresses the role that Iran has played in the dissemination of science and learning from the early Islamic period to the 'pre-Turkish' Seljuq period. Richter-Bernburg takes the reader on a journey from the Straits of Gibraltar to the Indus. He describes how the works of medical practitioners and scholars of Islamic Iran reached Europe through an Arabic-speaking world. He includes fascinating accounts about the contributions of outstanding scientists such as Razi and Avicenna who, despite their Iranian background, wrote in Arabic which was the 'privileged language of scholarship' during that time. The earliest textbook for medical practitioners and the earliest *materia medica* in Persian dates to the second half of the tenth century and originated first in eastern Iran. Persian only became the medium of medical language after the Seljuq Turkish conquest.

James Russell begins his chapter with a catalogue of the extant Zoroastrian texts in Book Pahlavi. These are mainly theological in content and, as Russell points out, do not tell us much about artistic and secular life during the Sasanian period (it might be noted here that the proliferation of religious literature three centuries after the Islamic conquest points to the continued existence of an active Zoroastrian priesthood, intent on preserving the old religion). In what he terms a 'silk-road of the intellect', Russell discusses the non-religious material that emerged in the early Islamic period and how it found its way into the literatures of other cultures via 'the newly-created Persian Muslims who committed themselves to preserving their old cultural treasures in a new tongue'. Russell shows how the literary tales and snatches of epic narrative, known to us in Arabic and Persian but poorly attested in Middle Persian, find parallels in the frescoes of Pandjikant. He compares this visual representation or 'miscellany' of cultural themes, enjoyed at home by wealthy Sogdian merchants, with the Armenian miscellany, or compendium of tales that became known by their title story: *History of the City of Brass*. Through the extraordinary confluence of literary themes that emerge in this text, Russell traces a complex pattern of cross-cultural contacts suggesting a 'polyphony in the presentation of literary characters, one that is neither linear nor hierarchic, with a din of different social, ethnic and religious voices acting upon each other'.

Robert Hillenbrand focuses on the theme of the Sasanian hunt in early Islamic art, from 637 to 1055 – up until the arrival of the Seljuk Turks. He regards the first four centuries of Islam as 'the dark age' in Iranian art, with the seat of power having been removed from Iran and shifted to the west. Hillenbrand admits that too little has survived to allow us to form a reliable image of artistic developments in the early period. He suggests that meanings attached to ancient traditions change over time; but memories survive, albeit in new forms, and ancient imagery takes on new meaning. The large hunting scenes of the Sasanian reliefs, as seen on the grotto of Taq-i Bustan in Kermanshah, and images of the Sasanian king as the hunter depicted on silver vessels loose their 'triumphant virtual vocabulary' in Islamic art. Such scenes as are found on a number of early Islamic textile fragments and the iconography suggests that the hunting theme is borrowed from unknown ancient traditions which are no longer fully understood. Hillenbrand argues that the artists borrowed from the past, but integrated the imagery with their own vision: '...these were also images of royal majesty and power which proved surprisingly resilient, and which could triumph over numerous mistakes of detail and balance'.

It is beyond the scope of seven contributions to cover all aspects of this crucial period in Iranian history and culture. However, the importance of this volume lies in the extraordinary diversity of subject matter and depth of observation presented by each scholar. A coherent theme emerges from the papers included in this collection which addresses the 'Idea of Iran' and the survival of its identity at a time when profound changes were taking place both politically and with respect to religion.

1

Re-emergence of Iranian Identity after Conversion to Islam

Ehsan Yarshater
(Columbia University)

The conversion of Iranians to Islam marks the greatest watershed in the history of the land and its people. In a series of battles, the Sasanian forces were defeated by the invading Arab Muslims, a ragged army driven by a new faith and much heartened by the prospect of booty from the prosperous Iranian cities and settlements. Ctesiphon, or Madāen, the Sasanian capital, fell in 637 CE, five years after the death of the Prophet. The defeat of the Persians at Nehavand five years later in 642 CE, which the Arabs called *Fatḥ al-futūḥ* 'the supreme victory,' sealed the fate of the Sasanian dynasty, and all hopes of effective resistance against the emboldened Arab army vanished. Yazdigird III fled east with his large retinue and treasures, and was murdered soon after, in 651 CE, at the instigation of Mahoy, a Persian grandee. The powerful Sasanian monarchy had come to an end after more than 400 years of effective rule.

Soon after the fall of the dynasty, the process of conversion began: Zoroastrian temples gradually gave way to mosques, and Allah replaced Ahura Mazdā as the creator of the world, while Satan assumed the role of Ahriman as the arch-tempter. Sasanian dualism gave way to the strictly monotheistic faith of Islam. The four elements, fire, water, earth and air, ceased to be sacred and people could now wash themselves in water and bury their dead in the earth instead of exposing them to wild beasts and birds of prey in *dakhma*s. Dogs, whose presence had been necessary in some Zoroastrian rites, eventually came to be regarded as ritually unclean. Daily prayers were said in Arabic while facing Mecca, often behind a prayer leader or *imām* in a mosque. The Qur'an was considered the word of God and the supreme authority on all matters, spiritual or otherwise. The words and deeds of the Prophet, as reported by his Companions and handed down to succeeding generations, supplemented the injunctions and provisions of the Qur'an. The large number of Zoroastrian deities, or *yazata*s, fell from their holy position, while Islamic archangels such as Gabriel, Michael, Esrafil, and Ezra'il came to prominence. The sun, the moon, and the stars lost their sanctified status. Friday became the weekly holy day, when congregational prayer was *de rigueur*, and a special sermon was delivered in the mosque in the name of the reigning caliph. Iran became part of the vast Islamic Empire, and Arab governors and their agents ruled the country.

The reasons and circumstances for the fall of the Sasanian monarchy, the victory of the Arabs, and the gradual process of conversion to Islam, have attracted much debate and a host of inter-related explicatory factors have been offered: the dissatisfaction and frustration of the population, caused by the abuses of power on the part of the Sasanian establishment, and the Zoroastrian clergy, the factionalism and rivalry of the upper most noble families, heavy taxes to finance repeated wars with Byzantium, especially under Khusrau II (590–628 CE), and to meet the lavish expenditure of the royal court, as well as further impositions by local potentates and ruling families. It has been further noted that the egalitarian Mazdakite movement toward the end of the dynasty, which aimed at abolishing the privileges of the rich and powerful and establishing the rights of the poor, was symptomatic of an ailing society. The wide extent of the movement and the large following that it attracted become clear from the Mazdakite colouring of the various nationalistic and anti-Arab movements that sprang up after the Arab conquest.

However, none of these explanations goes to the heart of the matter. Most of them merely describe symptoms and point to prevailing circumstances and conditions. We need to probe for a more satisfactory reason to explain how a small group of relatively simple, poor and unsophisticated people managed to overcome a rich and powerful state, defeating its army and overrunning its territories. We need to come up with an explanation that will be applicable to similar cases.

In my view, the underlying cause of the conditions that prevailed at the end of the Sasanian period — so characteristic of a weakened and disintegrating society with no appetite for self-defense — is none but old age. This is a cause that is generally ignored and is hardly ever put forward as the primary reason for a society's cataclysmic failure of nerve. I suppose its simplicity and obviousness hide its significance.

Yet the fact remains that not only dynasties, like plants or individuals, grow old and wither and die, but cultures and societies, too, put on years, lose their vigour and become exhausted and disappear or else drift along as servile followers or clients of a younger, rising power or culture that establishes its domination and ascendance.

I hope the fact that dynasties and civilisations eventually weaken, decline and disappear does not need to be argued. The historian who first paid attention to this factor and delineated the process of the rise and fall of dynasties and civilisations was the celebrated Muslim historian Ibn Khaldūn. In the famous Introduction (*Prolegomenon*) to his *History* he carefully describes how the rise of a state (dynasty) or civilisation has, as a rule, a beginning among a primitive, rough and intrepid people who are bereft of cultural refinements but are fearless and are united in their fierce solidarity — '*asabiyya* as he calls it — and strong backing of their leaders. In time, if they are destined to develop a civilisation — because not all primitive peoples are so destined — they rise through military strength to a position of power, conquering some weakened societies. Once their dominion is established and they can afford leisure, they become productive in arts and crafts, literature and thought. But then there comes a time when the power and wealth they have accrued leads them to bathe in luxury and enjoy the amenities that their success has afforded them.[1]

They cease to be vigilant and audacious. Their erstwhile daring and bravery give way to cautious avoidance of risk and indulgence in a life of pleasure, while their creative energy subsides and their determination weakens to maintain the quality of their life against external attacks or internal erosion. The very qualities that brought them to power are eventually squandered away and lost, and they become prey to a culturally younger and more determined, agile and adventurous people on the rise. Note that by the 'people' in this context is meant the elite of the society, i.e., those who manage the economic, political and cultural life of a society, while the masses follow their lead.

This cyclical view of history has also been advanced by some later historians, among them Giambattista Vico (d. 1744),[2] Oswald Spengler (d. 1936)[3] and Arnold Toynbee (d. 1975).[4] One should perhaps also consider Edward Gibbon (d. 1794)[5] among the believers in this theory, judging by the very title of his monumental *Decline and Fall of the Roman Empire*. To my knowledge no historian has described the conditions and features of declining cultures better than Toynbee in his *A Study of History* (Vol. V, pp. 11ff).

The pages of human history are, in fact, full of the accounts of the rise of certain peoples to prominence, their developing a specific culture, growing in power, producing their own brand of art and literature and then beginning to decline and being defeated by the invasion of younger people — I mean younger in cultural age — eager to gain power and nurture a culture of their own. Were it otherwise, we should be witnessing today the continued existence of Sumerian, Egyptian, Akkadian, Babylonian and Assyrian cultures. Were it otherwise, the brilliant Greek culture would have continued to this day and the great Roman civilisation would have preserved its strength rather than being destroyed in the fifth century by the invading 'barbaric' Germanic tribes. What happened, one may ask, to the ingenious legal system and the efficient administrative apparatus of the Romans? We may also ask what happened to India's distinctive art and philosophical thought or to Chinese initiatives in different fields and their remarkable Confucian system of training civil servants. Great civilisations, whether in Mesopotamia, Egypt, Syria, Anatolia, Persia, India or China or among the Incas, Mayas, or Aztecs, all eventually reached old age, weakened, suffered from inner exhaustion and were finally overwhelmed by younger rising peoples. If the pre-Columbian peoples had not exhausted their potentialities, they would not have been defeated by a small band of Spaniards who had sailed from thousands of miles away.

In Iran, the Sasanian monarchy with its courtly culture and royal authority reached its *nadir* after Khusrau II. This decline of the Iranians happened to coincide with the rise of the Arabs of Hejaz whose *'asabiyya* had received an invigorating impetus from a new, national faith, Islam.

But was this the last chapter in the annals of Iranian civilisation? Not so. The rise of the Persians in Khorasan and Transoxania in the eighth and ninth centuries CE and the subsequent flowering of Persian culture to an unprecedented degree, point to the fact that the defeat by the Arabs and conversion to Islam did not mean an end to Iranian cultural energy and political muscle. The effective rise of the Persians began with the activities of Abu Muslim, leading to the downfall of the Umayyad caliphate and the installation of the Abbasid caliphs that Jāḥiẓ, the famous Arab author and *adab* scholar, calls a 'Persian caliphate' (he calls the Umayyad caliphate *shāmiyya* and the Abbasid caliphate *'ajamiyya*).[6] This was followed by the rise of autonomous Persian dynasties of the Taherids, the Samanids and the Saffarids in eastern Iran, and the Deylamites in the north, all within the Islamic oecumene. The Buyids even ruled Baghdad effectively for more than a century, from 945 to 1055 CE and were appointing Abbasid caliphs for a while.[7] These all point to a renewed inner strength, capable of political assertion and cultural renewal.

The history of the Persian renaissance under the Samanids is too well known to require rehearsal. The important and surprising point is that in spite of conversion to Islam, despite some 200 years of strict Arab rule and in spite of Persian strides towards developing and consolidating Islam and the Islamic civilisation, Persia was the one country that, in contrast to Iraq, Syria and Egypt, was able to maintain its separate identity within the Islamic world, best expressed by the retention of the Persian language. The countries I have just mentioned were all heirs to magnificent ancient civilisations, but once they were conquered by the Arabs and had adopted Islam, they quickly shed their former identity, abandoned their original language, adopted Arabic as their vernacular and assumed forthwith an Arab identity — an identity that they have kept ever since. Indeed, by the time the Arab Muslims invaded their lands, the exhaustion and decay of their former strength and civilisation were complete. The importance of language, which is the vehicle for the narration of history and legend and expression of literary arts, cannot be overestimated. Through the Persian language, Iran remained connected to its past history and culture. The remembrance of the past and attachment to its culture were crystallised in Firdausi's *Shāhnāma*, which continued to inform and remind the Persians of their national heritage and their heroic age. The fact that the traditional history of Persia was largely mythical and legendary made no difference. To Iranians it *was* history and a perennial source of pride and inspiration. It confirmed their national identity.

The effervescence of cultural energy in Iran during the early centuries of Islam was vigorous enough not only to establish a new and distinct Iranian identity within the Islamic world but also to affect the neighboring nations and educate and absorb the invading nomads who kept pouring into Iran from Central Asia, whether they were the inexhaustible Turkish tribes or the numerous Mongol and Tartar hordes. The Persification of the Ghaznavids, the Seljuqs, the Khwarazmshahids, the Mongols, the Atābeks, the Timurids, the Aq-qoyulus and Qara-qoyulus or, for that matter, the Safavid Qizilbāsh tribes, the Afshars and the Qajars, and fashioning them into proponents and propagators of Persian language and culture in Central Asia, Anatolia and India testifies to the strength of this new culture despite the debilitation and decay that Iran had suffered towards the end of the Sasanian period. There is some truth in the saying that Persian language and culture travelled far and wide and influenced many nations by the grace of the sharp blades of the Turks, the Mongols and the Tartars. Yet, Persian language and culture could not have traversed so many regions had it not possessed alluring and persuasive qualities of its own. The decline and the political and cultural fatigue of Iranian society at the end of the Sasanian period thus proved temporary, not permanent.

This observation leads us to a second rule of the rise and decline of civilisations and societies. The decline of a dynasty or of a society need not necessarily mean a total and final exhaustion as happened in Egypt at the time of the Arab invasion or in Rome with the invasion of the Germanic tribes. We have to distinguish between total decay, at which point a people fall headlong into permanent decline, unable ever to recover again, and a temporary exhaustion when a society may suffer setbacks and be trounced by some energetic invaders, but after a period in the doldrums rises again and persevere for a while with renewed vigour until it comes to the final and ultimate end of its political and cultural energy.

And so it was that, overcome by Alexander's army, Iran suffered a temporary decline at the end of the Achaemenid period. But about a hundred years later, the Arsacids in the northeast, fresh from the Central Asian steppes, introduced a new corps of elite and began to inject new, invigorating life into Iranian society. They not only drove the Seleucids, i.e., Alexander's successors, out of the country, but were later able to stop the further encroachment of the Roman Empire eastward and became a worthy challenger to Rome, succeeding in a number of battles against the Roman army.

However, the Arsacid dynasty, in spite of its longevity, did not escape the rule. It deteriorated towards the end of the second century. The capture of its capital in Mesopotamia more than once by Roman emperors was symptomatic of its weakening and decline. Even if only half of the accusations that were levelled by the Sasanians against the Arsacids are true, it points to a situation not unlike that which prevailed at the end of the Sasanian period.

But this erosion of the political and cultural vigour, too, proved to be a transient one as the national malaise gave the opportunity to Ardashir, a young ruler in Fars, the homeland of the Achaemenids, to embark on a rebellion against the declining Arsacids, remove them, and start a new period of ambitious and energetic government with attendant cultural achievements.

Thus, Iran had experienced three periods of temporary exhaustion and decline before a new surge of inner strength gave the country a new and distinct identity within the Islamic world.

You hardly find a nation, with the exception of China, that in the course of its history has fallen so many times and then arisen again, phoenix-like from its ashes, with a show of new vigour and creativity. In this, Iran has been helped, contrary to the common perception, by a series of invasions, mostly from the plains of Central Asia. It is true that the Turkic nomads, the Mongols and the Tartars, the Arabs before them, and the Sakas, the Hephthalites and the Kidarites in pre-Islamic times, who invaded Iran, wrought great havoc and caused extensive destruction, but at the same time they injected fresh blood into the veins of the Iranians, providing them with a new source of inner energy. They were like a new graft on the trunk of an aged tree. Were it not for these fresh supplies of young blood, one may speculate that Iran would not have lasted as long as it has.

The astonishing endurance of Persian culture and identity may have been helped by other factors. For instance, Xavier de Planhol, a leading geographer of our time with profound and extensive knowledge of the Middle East and North Africa, and for years the Head of the Department of Geography at the Sorbonne, has also taken note of the fact that Iran preserved its identity, in spite of conversion to Islam and despite the rule of Turkish dynasties for so many centuries. In contrast, he mentions the case of Asia Minor, which was turkified and called Turkey a single century after the battle of Manzikert in 1071 that opened the gate of Anatolia to Turkish tribes.[8]

In his substantial work, *Les Nations du Prophète*, de Planhol notes the singularity of the Iranians in coping with Arab and Turkish domination.[9] He seeks the reason for the continued survival of Iran as a distinct culture in its system of agriculture. According to him, the survival of Iranian identity resulted from the technically advanced system of irrigation, and particularly the *qanāt* system, which allowed for the distribution of water through subterranean canals over long distances. The system gave a remarkable stability to Persian life based on agriculture. This stability, which was also reflected in Persian culture, continued during the repeated nomadic invasions of Iran, enabling the country to absorb and educate the nomads in the ways of Persian life and culture. A certain similarity between this theory and that of Karl Wittfogel, expressed in his *Oriental Despotism*, which takes the maintenance of irrigation systems as determining the social and political features of Oriental countries, is noticeable.

My own line of thinking follows a different path. To my mind, the simple process of aging is the villain behind the periodic or permanent deterioration and disintegration of societies and cultures. As noted before, we need to find a universal rule, applicable not only to Iran but to all similar cases throughout human history as well. Obviously, what I have called the exhaustion of inner strength or creative energy by old age and the time factor needs to be explained ultimately by biological processes. But it is not possible to offer a convincing biological explanation with the present state of our knowledge of genetics.

To sum up, the decline of the Sasanian dynasty and the depletion of Iranian political and cultural stamina, which led to the defeat at the hands of the Arab Muslims, did not mean that Persian cultural energy and creative strength had been exhausted for good, as was the case with a number of countries in the Middle East and North Africa. When we look at Iran some 250 years after the

Islamic conquest, we find the country at the threshold of a great renaissance and a brilliant cultural renovation. We find that Iran succeeds in asserting its distinct identity and is on the way to giving birth to the finest poetry and the most exquisite forms of decorative arts in its entire history. It is in this period that Iran produces its greatest epic poem, Firdausi's *Shāhnāma* its most engaging odes in Farrokhi's, Manuchehri's and Anvari's panegyrics, its outstanding romances in *Vis o Ramin* and in Nezami's *mathnavi*s, its most profound mystical poetry in 'Attar and Rumi's works, its most eloquent love lyrics in Sa'di's *ghazal*s and, the apogee of this genre, in the unparalleled *ghazal*s of Hafez.

Is Iran going to experience yet another revival of its cultural strength and creative vigour? This is a question that only the future can tell.

Notes:

1. *Muqaddimah* II, 1967: 278, 280-299, 344-345, 353-355 (the pages of the Arabic original are indicated in the translation).
2. Vico 1744: translation as in Bergin and Fisch 1948, §915:335.
3. Spengler 1919-22: 2 vols.; translation as in Atkinson 1926-28.
4. Toynbee 1934-61:12 vols.
5. Gibbon1844-45, The Decline and Fall of the Roman Empire.
6. Jaḥiẓ III: 366; see also Hovannisian and Sabagh 1998: 66ff.
7. See Cahen EI^2: 1350-1353.
8. de Planhol 1993: 480-481.
9. *Ibid.*

2

Survival of Iranianness

Hugh Kennedy
(School of Oriental and African Studies,
University of London)

Why is Iran not an Arab country? At first sight this seems a simple, perhaps even slightly absurd question. Everyone knows that Iranians speak Persian, a non-Arabic, non-Semitic language, that Iran has an ancient and distinctive history of which its people are proud and that Iranians have a strong sense of national identity and national pride. A more considered look at the historical background, however, suggests that the survival of Iranianness through the Arab conquests was not inevitable but the result of the nature of the conquest and the varieties of different relationships which grew up between the Arab rulers and their Iranian subjects.

To bring out the exceptional nature of the Iranian trajectory, it is fruitful to compare its history with that of other areas conquered by the Arabs at the same time. In 632 CE, the year of the death of the Prophet Muhammad, there were some Arabic speakers in Syria and Iraq, mostly along the desert margins but some in towns like Damascus and Hira in Iraq. The majority of the population of both areas spoke Greek in Syria, Pahlavi (Middle Persian) in Iraq or dialects of Aramaic in both. In Egypt there were virtually no resident Arabic speakers and in the Maghreb Arabs were almost completely unknown. In the east too, we can be confident that there were no Arabic speakers in Iran, with the possible exception of some small communities along the Persian Gulf coast. In this paper, I want to investigate the problem why Iran retained its linguistic and cultural identity in the face of the Arab onslaught when Iraq, Syria, Egypt and the lands to the west became almost completely Arabised. The survival of Berber identity in the Maghreb lies beyond the scope of this paper.

The survival of Persian language and culture was the result of the continuation of a self-consciously Iranian elite many of whose members were committed to the maintenance of Iranian traditions. This elite flourished both outside and inside the formal structures of early Islamic government. Outside, some members of this elite ruled the small semi-independent principalities to be found in the more remote and mountainous areas of the Iranian world where the spirit and customs of pre-Islamic Iran were maintained for centuries after the Muslim conquest. Other members of the elite worked, so to speak, within the system, bringing Iranian cultural values to the Arab-Muslim administration of the caliphate.

Iranianness survived most obviously in the development of the new Persian language which from the tenth century becomes a language of administration and literary high culture and from the eleventh century a language of philosophy and science.[1] The continued respect for the memory and administrative legacy of the Sasanian *shāhānshāh* is also central. Attempts by the direct descendants of Yazdigird III, the last Persian king to re-establish the monarchy were sporadic and unsuccessful. However, most of the Persianate dynasts of the late ninth and tenth centuries made efforts to claim descent from the old royal house or from other prominent figures in Sasanian history. Along with this went the preservation of Persian administrative ideals. The virtuous circle by which the ruler looks after the peasantry who provide the resources to fund the army which in turn protects the peasants is a characteristically Sasanian formulation repeated in early Islamic political philosophy. The image of the wise and powerful vizier, understanding the style and technicalities of administration, mediating the impulses and anger of the ruler is again a Persian administrative topos. But the point goes further than the simple importation of administrative devices: it is about the wider respect for Iranian political norms as a worthy and admirable model. From court ceremonial to the collection of taxes at a village level, Sasanian practice was accepted and adopted. This cultural self-confidence, so characteristic of the Iranian elite in the early Islamic period, reaches its triumphant conclusion in Firdausi's *Shāhnāma* of c. 1000 CE, a vast hymn to the glories of the past and an assertion of the relevance of that past to the present and the future.[2]

This adherence to Iranian values was seldom directly connected to attempts to preserve and revive the old Zoroastrian state religion and such attempts as were made were entirely unsuccessful. Much more important was the process by which Iranian elites adopted and adapted Islam. The fundamental importance of this was that it meant that men could maintain the old Persian cultural and political traditions without laying themselves open to the charge of being infidels and leaving them vulnerable to Muslim *jihad.*

Some of the most obvious examples of the survival of Iranian political and cultural identities can be found in the small principalities which survived on the peripheries of the caliphate. In the more remote areas, separated from the main centres of Arab authority by desert wastes or steep mountain ranges, local polities survived almost unaffected by the coming of the new rulers. These areas were nominally 'conquered' by the Arabs in the seventh or early eighth centuries but in reality Arab armies never established control in the first century of Islam and neither Muslim missionaries nor Arab settlers ever penetrated on any significant scale.

Typical of these areas were the mountain principalities of Gilan and Tabaristan at the south end of the Caspian Sea. Here princes with ancient Iranian titles like Ispahbad ('commander of the army' in Middle Persian administrative usage) and claiming descent from the Sasanian elite continued to rule, their power and authority undimmed in exchange for a simple tribute payment to the Muslim authorities, a tribute which they collected in the way that they chose.[3]

There were two lines of Ispahbads of Tabaristan that we know about. The first, conventionally known as the Dabuyids appear as local governor for the Sasanian *shah*s in Gilan. After the initial Arab conquest they expanded eastwards to Tabaristan. They were protected by the rugged terrain of their kingdom. The mountains of northern Iran rise with dramatic suddenness from the plains to the south. The great Khorasan road which led from Iraq, through Hamadan, Ray and Nishapur to distant Marv, the capital of Khorasan in the early Islamic period, skirted the southern edge of the range, but Arab armies passed by, untempted by the meagre booty to be obtained from these mountain people and deterred by the steep terrain, bleak and exposed on the south, jungly and treacherous on the north. The Ispahbads acted as independent players in the politics of early Islamic Iran, allying themselves, for instance, with Qutayba b. Muslim (governor of Khorasan, 705–15 CE) against his rival Yazīd b. al-Muhallab and when in 716–8 CE Yazīd attempted to conquer Tabaristan, he was soundly defeated by the forces of the Ispahbad, supported by Daylamites from the mountains to the west. Tabaristan grew rich from exporting textiles across the Caspian Sea to the peoples of Central Asia and the kings minted their own coins, not dated from the *hijra* as Islamic coins were, but from the era of the last Sasanian *shah* Yazdigird III.[4] The Dabuyid Ispahbads supported the rebellion of Sunbadh who attempted to avenge the murder of Abū Muslim by the Caliph al-Manṣūr and restore the Zoroastrian religion. After the defeat of his rebellion, the caliph was determined to punish them, and in 141 AH/758 CE Tabaristan was conquered and the last of the old line of princes, Khurshīd b. Dādmihr was driven out.

This conquest did not, however, mark the end of Iranian rule in Tabaristan. Arab governors were installed in the towns of Amol and Sari along the Caspian coast but the people of the high mountains remained effectively independent. In this area, the Dabuyid Ispahbads were replaced by another dynasty, the Bawandids. Claiming descent from the Sasanian *shah* Kavad, they maintained their rule for six or seven centuries, surviving the Mongol conquests until their final disappearance in the fourteenth century. Unlike the Dabuyids, the Bawandids converted to Islam, probably in the ninth century, and this conversion was one reason why they were able to maintain their power for so long but their regnal names betray their cultural affiliations: names like Shapur, Shahriyar, Rostam and Dara (Darius) were redolent with the glory and prestige of the old Persian monarchy.

Further to the east in the southern Caspian mountains lay the domains of another Iranian dynasty, the Karinvand who claimed descent from one Karen who, it was claimed, had been granted parts of Tabaristan by no less a person than the Khusrau I Anushirvan. In 166 AH/783 CE the leaders of these two dynasties, joined by another local lord with the evocative title of Masmughan ('Great One of the Magians') launched a major rebellion to drive the Muslims out. The local chronicles report that all the Muslims were massacred in a single day. It took major campaigns by Abbasid armies to reclaim some sort of suzerainty. The Karinid ruler Vindadhurmuzd was defeated and wounded and taken to Baghdad by the caliph Mūsā al-Hadi but it is noteworthy that he was soon allowed to return to his homeland and resume his old status.

Khwarazm lies at the south end of what used to be the Aral Sea, in the delta of the Oxus river. It is cut off from the south and west, the direction of Arab advance, by the grim wastes of the Karakum (Black Sand) desert. This was a very remote and separate land: they spoke and wrote their own Iranian language which sounded to the tenth century Muslim traveller Ibn Fadlan 'like the chattering of starlings'. It was ruled by a dynasty known as the Afrighids who had long held power in the area as vassals of the Sasanian *shah*s.[5] When the Arab-Muslim forces began to penetrate the lands beyond beyond the Oxus from 705 CE, they naturally took an interest in this rich area but the Arab 'conquest' consisted largely of supporting the reigning Afrighid against his ambitious brother. The king of Khwarazm became a vassal of the Arabs in the sense that he (probably, sometimes) paid a tribute to the authorities in Marv, but no Arab troops were stationed there and no Muslim missionaries prosyletised among the people. Until the coming of the Seljuq Turks in the eleventh century, the Afrighid kings ruled over what was socially and culturally an independent state, a state in which the monarchs proclaimed their legitimacy not by the will of Allah but by their descent from the Sasanian kings of old.

Tabaristan and Khwarazm are good and comparatively well attested examples of the survival of Iranian statelets through the early Islamic period but they were not the only ones. On the north-eastern fringes of the Islamic world, or that part of the world over which the Muslim government in Khorasan exercised some sort of hegemony, there were other state where princes of Iranian or Turco-Iranian origin, like the Afshins of Ustrushana or the Ikhshids of Ferghana exercised their sway in a way their fathers and grandfathers had done when Prophet Muhammad was wandering in the hills around Mecca receiving his first revelations. The case of the Afshins of Ustrushana is particularly interesting. One of them took service as a military leader with the Abbasid caliphs. After a distinguished career, he was arrested on a trumped up charge of apostasy from Islam and put on trial. The prosecution alleged that he was not a true Muslim; among other things he kept old religious books in jewelled cases, his subjects adored him as a god, as they had his ancestors before him, and he had punished Muslim missionaries who hade attempted to convert his people to Islam. A century and a half after the Arab 'conquest' of Transoxania, Afshin, though professedly a Muslim, was keeping state like any ancient Persian prince.

A peculiar example of the survival of Iranianness can be found in the history of the Shirvan *shah*s of the eastern Caucasus.[6] The use of the old Persian royal title proclaims their attachment to old Iranian values and they duly claimed descent from the great warrior king Bahram Gur (Bahram V). What makes their story so interesting, however, is the fact that they were not of

Iranian ancestry at all. The founder of the dynasty was a pure bred Arab, Yazīd b. Mazyad al-Shaybānī, whose family were renowned as 'knights of the Arabs' and personifications of traditional Bedouin values. Yazīd became governor of the Caucasus area. After his death in 185 AH/801 CE he was succeeded by his son Khālid and the governorate became effectively hereditary and independent. By the eleventh century CE they were using such characteristically Iranian names as Qubad, Manuchehr and Faridun. The fictional Iranian descent was clearly considered to be more valuable than real descent from one of the noblest Arab tribes.

In some ways it was the speed of the Arab conquest that allowed the survival of local power structure and elites. Arab settlement was very limited. Until the end of the Umayyad period, the only major settlement was in Marv, the capital of the northeastern province of Khorasan. There may have been a garrison at Isfahan but it was not substantial enough to have a major effect on the ethnic make-up of central Iran. In some areas we know that the Muslim 'conquest' amounted to little more than the rearranging of power among the local elite. In the strategic city of Ray, near modern Tehran, the Mihran family who had dominated urban life for much of the Sasanian period decided to resist the invaders but their main rivals, the Zinabis sent out peace feelers and arranged an alliance with the Arabs which resulted in the overthrow of Mihranid domination and the installation of the Zinabis as the leading power in the town.[7] Further west in Qom, the leader of the city saw the Arabs, not as hostile conquerors, but as potential allies to help defend the city and its territory against the depredations of the wild Daylamite people of the highlands to the north.[8]

Much of this cultural heritage was preserved by the Iranian landowners of Mesopotamia (modern Iraq). This was a society dominated by a Persian speaking, Zoroastrian elite while the bulk of the population were Aramaic speaking farmers, peasants and craftsmen.[9] In the aftermath of the initial Arab conquests, most of the higher aristocracy, the Sasanian ruling family, and the elite military connected with them abandoned their estates and followed the royal court of King Yazdigird III as he fled east to try to organise resistance. However many smaller Persian landowners, the class know as *dehqan*s, remained behind and came to terms with the new masters of the country. Al-Balādhurī gives a short list of *dehqan*s who converted to Islam in the immediate aftermath of the conquests, including Jamīl b. Buṣbuhrī, *dehqan* of al-Falālīj and al-Nahrayn, Bistām b. Narsī of Bābil and Khuṭarniya, al-Rufayl of al-'Āl and Fīrūz of Nahr al-Malik, and Kūthā and we are told that the caliph 'Umar left their lands in their hands and 'cancelled the poll-tax (*jizyā)* on their necks'.[10] He also reports that later, during the caliphate of 'Alī (656–61 CE), *dehqan*s who rode on horses (*barādhīn)* and wore gold rings on their legs (a mark of aristocratic status in Iranian society) had to pay a tax of 48 *dirham*s per year, twice as much as merchants who paid 24 and four times that rate for farmers (*al-akira)* and the rest who paid only twelve.[11] These were *dehqan*s who had not chosen to convert to Islam but who clearly preserved their wealth and social status. Because the Arabs settled in cities and lived off the proceeds of taxation, they had no desire to deprive these men of their position and status. On the contrary, they actually needed them to run the administrative system on which they depended for their living. A Persian-speaking landed elite survived the conquest in Iraq, maintaining their own cultural identity, and this *dehqanat* was a major factor in transmitting Sasanian Persians norms and values to the new Islamic state.

Something of the role and importance of the *dehqan*s of the fertile *Sawād* of lower Iraq can be seen in the story of the rise to power of al-Faḍl b. Sahl, vizier and chief adviser to the caliph al-Ma'mūn (813–33 CE) in his early years. He came from a family which had an estate *(day'a)* and house in the district of Sīb. The family remained Zoroastrians until the reign of Hārūn al-Rashīd and had clearly maintained their privileged status during the century and a half since the Muslim conquest. His grandfather rejoiced in the characteristically Iranian aristocratic name of Zādānfarrūkh. His uncle, who was head of the family, had prospered as an agent for a neighbouring landowner but he had incurred the jealousy of his employer who beat him to death in a drunken rage and took both house and estate. Sahl then went to seek redress from the Barmakid vizier Yaḥyā b. Khālid and it was then that the family first came into contact with prominent members of the administration. House and land restored, the young al-Faḍl took service with the Barmakids. He attracted the admiration of Yaḥyā for the elegance and fluency with which he translated a book from Persian *(fārisiya)* to Arabic. He rose to power, in fact, as a mediator of Persian culture to the Arab-Muslim elite. A vignette in the history of the period shows something of the values of the *dehqans*.[12] Ja'far, the princely young Barmakid, is riding through the Iraq countryside 'bareback wearing an embroidered robe *(jubba)*, no trousers, carrying an unsheathed sword'. Behind him rides a Magian *(majūsī)* 'with a long neck'. The Magian stops to ask the people standing by the road for a drink of water. They offer him water in a green pottery jug *(kūz)* but he is full of disdain: 'It seems to me that the *dehqanat* has almost disappeared so that no trace of it is left: where is the silver? Where is the glass?' and is told that they are forbidden by Islam and in the end he reluctantly agrees to drink out of the pottery jug. Of course, it would be wrong to suggest that all *dehqan*s and other Persians in Iraq followed this line. No doubt some fled and others converted to Islam but a sufficient number remained to become a forceful presence in the new state. Some Persian elite troops went over to the Muslim cause after the initial defeat of Persian armies at Qādisiya, but they too, retained their own separate identity. They fought alongside the Muslim armies but were not themselves converts to Islam and they fought in their own named units[13]. The Aramaean population, by contrast, maintained a very low profile. *Dehqan*s may have been proud of their Persian culture but there is little evidence that anyone was ever proud to preserve their Aramaean heritage.[14] In Iraq, in contrast to Syria, a 'gentry' class and a cultural heritage did survive the Muslim conquests but it was of Persian heritage, not an Aramaean one.

It is perhaps interesting to compare the survival of the *dehqanat* in Iraq with the fate of the gentry of Byzantine Egypt. We know that there was a rich landowning elite in pre-Islamic Egypt.[15] We know that because the affairs of families like the Apions[16] were documented in the papyri which means that we have a clearer idea of their personal and financial arrangements than we have for elite society in any other part of the late Antique world. The Apions disappear from the record, if not necessarily from the historical reality, in the early seventh century but we know from the evidence of early Islamic administrative papyri that Greek-speaking elite families continued to hold estates and conduct local administration through the Muslim conquests and well into the first century of Islamic rule. It is interesting that we know this because of the survival of the papyri which show how the local landowners of Middle Egypt continued to fulfil much the same roles as they had in Byzantine times. They look, in fact, very much like the *dehqan*s of early Islamic Iraq. And yet, something is missing. The existence of this class has left no trace in the Arabic historical literature. There is no equivalent of the *dehqanat*, that combination of administrative techniques and cultural values which was the legacy to the Iraqi Persian 'gentry' to the early Islamic state. No one in the early Islamic administration of Egypt took pride in their Greek/Egyptian background as the family of al-Faḍl b. Sahl did in Iraq and Iran. The Greek-speaking gentry of Egypt simply disappear from the record when Arabic becomes the language of administration in the early eighth century. This is not to say that the descendants of this gentry class did not convert to Islam and under their new Muslim names play a useful part in the bureaucracy of Islamic Egypt. The important point, however, is that they lost their identity: no one in Islamic Egypt claimed descent from the Apions or any of the other families who provided the pagarchs of Byzantine Egypt nor did they exhort the rulers to look back to the administration of Byzantine Egypt as a model. Again, in practice there was clearly a good deal of continuity between Byzantine and Islamic systems of local taxation but no one we know of held the Byzantine system up as an ideal to be followed nor did they proclaim that the cultural values of the Byzantine gentry where an ideal to be emulated.

It is worth speculating why there was this difference between the relative status of these two social groups. The first and most simple point is geographical. After the Abbasid revolution of 750 CE, the new caliphs settled in Iraq, the homelands of the *dehqan*s. Furthermore, the alluvial lands of central and southern Iraq were by far the most important contributors to the revenues of the caliphate. They therefore had the great advantage of proximity to the centre of power with the added bonus that this power was heavily dependent on their expertise to extract resources. By contrast the Greek-using gentry of early Islamic Egypt were close only to governors of a province whose terms of office were short and whose courts offered little in the way of patronage and career.

There may also be another factor to be reckoned with here, and one which I will come back to again, the overtly hereditary nature of status in the Iranian world. Power may have been effectively hereditary among the Byzantine gentry, indeed the long survival of the Apions suggests that to all intents and purposes it was, but this *de facto* heredity was not accompanied by an ideology of hereditary status. By contrast, the Sasanian world set a great deal of store on descent: it was a society in which ancestry, real or fictitious, was of enormous importance in determining social status. Unlike the Roman Empire, the Sasanian monarchy was unequivocally hereditary and the great families of the state were proud of their ancient lineages.

An interesting illustration of this can be seen in the biographical dictionaries of the early Islamic period. These vast compilations, often running to many thousand entries, were intended to help scholars check the identity of those who were said to have passed on traditions of the Prophet and hence to assess the validity of these tradition. Richard Bulliet used these dictionaries to produce an analysis of the rates on conversion to Islam.[17] He began with dictionaries from the Iranian world. He found that many entries traced the genealogy back to the pre-Islamic, Persian name of the ancestor. Assuming that this Persian named person was a non-Muslim, he then worked out the approximate period at which the family had converted to Islam. It is not the purpose of this paper to assess the reliability of Bulliet's work, though it must be said that while it was greeted with some initial scepticism, it has since become widely accepted. It is rather to note that the subjects of Bulliet's dictionary thought it important to remember their pre-Islamic identities. Having worked through the Iranian material, Bulliet then sought to expand his work to include biographies from Iraq and all points west as far as Muslim Spain. But here he came up against a problem. None of the entries for these areas went back to a named pre-Islamic member of the family. In the event, Bulliet used the prevalence of certain patterns of Muslim naming to giving some idea about the timing of conversion. For the purposes of this paper, however, the important point to notice is that virtually none of the subjects of these dictionaries, tens of thousands of them, thought it important to preserve the memory of their pre-Islamic ancestry: for them, the importance of the family began with the coming of Islam and their was no status or prestige to be derived from tracing their ancestry to Byzantine Syria or Visigothic Spain. The contrast is stark and striking, and surely suggestive.

These survivals of the political and social elites of pre-Islamic Iran were marked by a parallel process of conversion to the new elite religion. The most famous and best documented example of this process is to be found in the family history of the Barmakids.[18] The title of Barmak was born by the hereditary guardians of the great Buddhist shrine of Naubahar, which lay outside the walls of the ancient city of Balkh, now in northern Afghanistan. Although they were Buddhists, not Zoroastrians, the family seem to have been thoroughly Iranianised. Barmak was said to have converted to Islam at the hands of Asad b. 'Abdallāh the then Umayyad governor of Khorasan who ruled from 723–27 and 735–38 CE. His son then took the Arab Muslim name of Khālid and subsequent generations were known by a Muslim first name but also by their family name of al-Barmaki. Khalid joined the Abbasid movement at an early stage and made a very successful career as a financial administrator:

his sons and grandsons went on to become the famous family of viziers under the Abbasid caliphs. The story of the Barmakids and their dramatic fall in 803 CE is too well-known to rehearse here, but certain points should be noted. The Barmak who was said to have been converted at the hands of the Umayyad governor. Asad b. ʻAbdallāh was a governor with a consistent policy of making links with the local elites and this was, in fact, an elite conversion, the highest ranking member of the Arab-Islamic community welcoming Barmak to join them. However, there were problems and the family seems to have abandoned the Naubahar. At the time of the Abbasid revolution, Khālid b. Barmak joined the rebel armies and attracted the attention of the caliphs by his administrative talents. The Barmakids went on to become the greatest administrative dynasty in the caliphate. What is striking about the Barmakid story is that they gloried in their Persian culture heritage. They were converts to Islam, and probably sincere Muslims, but they also looked back with pride to the greatness of the old Persian empire and brought culture values and administrative practices from that world to the service of the new.

Despite the fact that many of the Persian elite converted to Islam at an early stage, Iran was the only part of the Muslim world in which there were major anti-Muslim uprisings in the early Islamic period.[19] On at least two occasions there were clear attempts to overthrow the new religion by force. The Abbasid revolution which began in Khorasan in 747 CE was ostensibly a Muslim movement and there can be little doubt that most of those who joined the anti-Umayyad armies sincerely wanted to establish a more perfectly Islamic state. However, not everyone who took up arms shared these views. In the years immediately after the victory of the Abbasids, one Sunbādh, who had supported the Abbasid claim, raised a rebellion which had, according to the Muslim chroniclers, a clear anti-Islamic character. He and his followers were to drive the Muslims out and go on to sack Mecca in revenge for the destruction of Zoroastrian temples.[20] The movement was suppressed, with great loss of life, but its existence is a clear indication of the sentiments of at least some of the population of northeast Iran. Almost two centuries later, a Daylamite warlord, Mardāvīj b. Ziyār made a vigorous attempt to restore the old religion in western Iran.[21] Like many other Iranian princes, he claimed descent from the old Persian nobility, in this case the kings of Gīlān in the time of the mythical *shah* Kay Khusrau. He stressed his role as a would be heir to the Sasanians when he ordered that the great palace of Khusrau, the Tāq-i Kisrā southeast of Baghdad should be restored and made ready for him. Like Sunbādh before him, Mardāvīj failed, being killed in his bath by Turkish soldiers in 935 CE and none of his contemporaries took up the challenge. The Daylamites who came to dominate western Iran and Iraq were all professed Muslims. Their eventual failure should not lead us to underestimate the exceptional nature of these movements. Apart from Berber North Africa, there was nowhere else in the lands conquered by the Arabs in the century after Muhammad's death, where a clear attempt to challenge the dominance of Islam was made. It is also interesting that it was clearly linked to the restoration of the old political order.

If attempts to restore the pre-Islamic religion of Iran were unsuccessful, the Iranians of the ninth and tenth centuries CE had other ideological props to justify their position. They developed a distinctively Persian administrative tradition and they adumbrated a new high culture.

Persian administrative practice was highly regarded in the early Islamic state, especially at the Abbasid court. At one level this high regard was a reflection of the practical achievements of the administrators. The early Abbasid state was heavily dependent on the revenues of the *Sawād* of Iraq, the area which had been known as *dil Iranshahr*, the heart of Iran, and had provided much of the revenues of the Sasanian state. Both Umayyads and Abbasids needed to expertise of men who knew and understood the fiscal systems and geographies of the *Sawād*. Naturally most of these, especially in the early years after the conquest, were Iranians who had been fulfilling the same functions under Persian rule. Al-Jahshiyari, writing in the early fourth AH/tenth century CE begins his history of the viziers of the early caliphs with an admiring account of the administration of the Sasanian monarchs as it was remembered in his time.[22] He also takes care to emphasise the respect in which the kings held administrators and the science of administration. The implication is that Persian practice was the origin of Islamic practice and an example to be followed by all conscientious bureaucrats. As already noted, however, the governors of Egypt in the first century CE were heavily dependent on Greek-speaking administrators in the Egyptian countryside but these administrators did not succeed in securing a high status for Greek administrative practice. Nobody in the early Islamic world openly looked back to the administrative achievements of Justinian, or any other Emperor, and held them up as examples how things ought to be done. In contrast, however, Justinian's Sasanian contemporary Khusrau Anushirvan, 'the just' was widely celebrated as the exemplar of the perfect ruler. Despite the fact that he was not a Muslim (clearly), he is used by that arch-Persian bureaucrat, Niẓām al-Mulk to explain how good rulers should function.

If Muslims respected Persian administrative practice, they were also impressed by Persian royal style. The Tāq-i Kisrā lay only a few kilometres from Baghdad, its vast size making a mockery of any attempts by Muslim rulers to challenge it. There were of course mighty Roman ruins and Baalbek, Palmyra and numerous other classical sites in Syria but they came from a world too far removed from the consciousness for medieval Muslims to be any sort of example or inspiration or to validate the culture which had constructed them, and their construction was often ascribed to Solomon or the *jinn* rather than Roman rulers. The Tāq-i Kisrā, by contrast, was known to be the palace of the Sasanian *shah*s whose identities and exploits were well known. It might have been bigger and more magnificent than any Muslim palace, but it belonged to a recognisable genre of building for a king.

The history of pre-Islamic Iran was integrated into the classical Arabic tradition in a way which was only paralleled by the biblical narratives. This 'history' was not entirely the history of pre-Islamic Iran as we understand it today. The medieval Islamic world knew nothing of the Achaemenians. They saw the mighty ruins of Persepolis but they ascribed them to the mythical king Jamshid who had first ordered the world or to Solomon whose miraculous powers were always respected. 'Real' history begins with the invasion of Alexander and his defeat of Dara (Darius) the only one of the ancient kings actually named.

The Seleucid and Parthian kings, *mulūk al-tawā'if*, hardly figure but the Sasanians loom extremely large. The Sasanian court had generated, in some way that we do not quite understand, a chronicle of history called the *Khwadāy nāmag* or 'book of lords'. A version was translated into Arabic and incorporated into Tabarī's great *History of the Prophets and Kings*, the most important collection of early Islamic historical writing. In this way the memory of the Sasanian monarchs was kept alive in Arab Muslim historiography. The kings and heroes of the epoch were widely known and respected. There were wise, just and noble rulers like Anushirvan, brave rebels and mighty hunters like Bahram Gur, a whole range of characters and incidents which became part of *adab*, the canon of knowledge and polite learning which any aspiring courtier or intellectual could be expected to have at his finger tips. No such information was collected about the identities and deeds of Roman rulers: Caesar, Constantine and Justinian were no more than names in lists, if that. They had no prestige, no cultural value in the Arab Muslim tradition and provided no models to which the Syrians or Egyptians could look to validate their own historical identities. Persians could, and did, boast of the achievements of their non-Muslim forebears, the descendants of the Greek-speaking inhabitants of the former Byzantine lands had no such cultural capital to draw on, no ancestors (real or imagined) of whom they could be proud.

It was the combination of the political and social survival of important elements of the old Iranian elite with the possession of this cultural self-confidence which lay at the heart of the survival of Iranian national identity. More than anything else, it was the generation of New Persian poetry and historiography which confirmed this cultural identity. New Persian emerges from Middle Persian as French does from late Latin. It is a recognisably cognate language and many of the words from basic and every day objects are related. However, it marks a departure in several ways. The most obvious of these is that it uses the Arabic script with a few additional letters. It also incorporates a considerable number of Arabic words, mostly for the types of administrative, judicial and philosophical concepts, the sort of abstract nouns for which English turns to Latinate roots. This led to the development of a language which was easy to read and write, versatile and effective with a vocabulary large enough to express the most difficult abstruse ideas. The language spread, particularly in the lands to the north and east of the heartlands of Iran. The Muslim conquests had broken down the barriers which had separated these lands from the Sasanian Empire and regional Iranian languages like Sogdian and Khwarezmian disappeared. Apart from a small number of towns on the main roads, Nehavand, Qom and Nishapur for example, where there was a substantial Arab settlement and where Arabic was generally spoken, New Persian became the *lingua franca* of Muslim Iran and the dialect known as *darī* or court language became the main medium of polite and political discourse. *Darī*, in one form or another, was probably the language of the majority of the Khorasani soldiers who followed Abū Muslim in 747–50 CE and brought the Abbasids to power.

There is a famous, and possibly apocryphal, story about the emergence of the first New Persian poetry. The scene is set at the court of the rough and ready ruler of Sistan, Yā‘qūb b. Layth in 865 CE. Sistan was a remote province on what is now the desolate borderland between Iran and Afghanistan. Until Tamerlane's conquest at the end of the fourteenth century, this was a comparatively wealthy area, with old established cities and a rich agricultural economy based on the inland delta of the Helmand river. It was also the homeland of the great mythical hero Rostam and his horse Rakhsh, whose tomb was still shown to medieval travellers: a centre, in fact, of old Iranian lore. The scene is set when Yā‘qūb has just won a notable victory over his local rival and the court poets set out to eulogise him in Arabic, as was the custom at this time. Yā‘qūb complained that he could not understand the verses and one of his secretaries, Muhammad b. Vasīf set out to produce the first New Persian poetry. The anecdote is significant in a number of ways. The *mise en scène* is a court one, the language of panegyric must be a court language, not the language of popular song but at the same time, it must be as widely comprehensible as possible. The anecdote is reported in the *Ta'rīkh-i Sistān*, the first works of New Persian prose literature and it is significant that the poetry is said to have emerged in eastern Iran, where there was not only less Arab influence but also less competition from Middle Persian, which was still used by the Zoroastrian religious hierarchy in Fars. By the mid-ninth century CE, New Persian was emerging as a court language.

It was no accident therefore that this New Persian court poetry reached its first flowering in the court of the Samanids in Bukhara in the tenth century CE. The Samanids were a dynasty whose origins were to be found among the landowning *dehqan*s of what is now northern Afghanistan, though, naturally, they claimed descent from the Sasanian royal house. They were said to have converted to Islam at the same time as the Barmakids but, unlike the latter, they remained in the northeast of the Muslim world and eventually established themselves as rulers in Transoxania. It seems to have been a deliberate part of their court policy to generate a New Persian court culture. Poets of the Samanid court like Rudaki (d. 329 AH/940–1 CE) and the first epic poet Daqiqi (d. c. 370 AH/980 CE) established the classic forms. Equally important was the free translation of the great history of al-Tabarī into New Persian by the vizier Abū ‘Alī Bal‘amī in about 352 AH/963–4 CE on the orders of the then Samanid ruler Manṣūr b. Nūḥ.

By the end of the Samanid period (the last ruler was killed in 395 AH/1005 CE) a mature New Persian court culture had been developed. This was brought to a triumphant climax in the *Shāhnāma* of Firdausi (d. between 1020 and 1025

CE). He came from the landowning *dehqanat* of Khorasan and worked under the patronage of the Ghaznavids, a dynasty of Turkish military origins who nonetheless patronised Persian culture. The *Shāhnāma* is crucially important because it tells the story of the ancient kings of Persia in the New Persian language. The importance of this work for the preservation and development of Iranian national consciousness cannot be exaggerated. In simple forceful language, comprehensible to all, it told the story of ancient Persian greatness. The Persians were equipped with an origin myth and cultural paradigm which they could defend against all comers.

Towards the end of Firdausi's work, he includes a verse letter which he claims was sent by Rostam, commander of the Persian army which attempted, unsuccessfully, to defend Iraq from Arab invasions in 636 CE, to his brother. There is no reason to assume that the letter is what it claims to be or that it dates from the seventh century CE but it is nonetheless interesting for the attitudes it expresses. Part of it is essentially a prophecy expressing Rostam's vision of the consequences of the Muslim conquest and it is extremely interesting in showing how an aristocratic Persian of Firdausi's time saw the coming of the Muslims.[23] He does not explicitly condemn Islam or the Arabs, but he paints a sorrowful view of the consequences of the conquest for traditional Iranian culture and values. The disruption of the old social order caused by the coming of Islam leads to the decay of public and personal morality.

He begins section with a general lament:

> But when the pulpit's equal to the throne
> And Abu Bakr and Umar's names are known
> Our long travails will be as naught, and all
> The glory we have known will fade and fall

He then comments on the general drabness of Muslim rulers compared with the splendour of the old courts of the King of Kings. It is interesting to see how his comments on the austerity of Muslim dress are the mirror image of those Arabic narratives of the conquests which glory in their virtuous poverty and contrast it with Persian luxury.

> They'll dress in black[24], their headdresses will be made
> Of twisted lengths of silk or black brocade
> There'll be no golden boots or banners then
> Our crowns and thrones will not be seen again

It will be an era of injustice and oppression and the collapse of the old social order:

> Some will rejoice while others live in fear
> Justice and charity will disappear
> Strangers will rule us then and with their might
> They'll plunder us and turn our days to night

They will not care for just or righteous men
Deceit and fraudulence will flourish then.
Warriors will go on foot, while puffed-up pride
And empty boasts will arm themselves and ride;
The peasantry will suffer from neglect
Lineage and skill will garner no respect
Men will be mutual thieves and have no shame
What's hidden will be worse than what is known
And stony-hearted kings will seize the throne.
No man will trust his son and equally
No son will trust his father's honesty

Moral standards will decay and this will go along with the decay of court culture.

Men will conceal their wealth, but when they've died,
Their foes will pillage everything they hide.
Men will pretend they're holy or they're wise,
To make a livelihood by telling lies.
Sorrow and anguish, bitterness and pain
Will be as happiness was in the reign
Of Bahram Gur[25] – mankind's accustomed fate:
There'll be no feasts, no festivals of state,
No pleasures, no musicians, none of these:
But there'll be lies, and traps and treacheries.
Sour milk will be our food, coarse cloth our dress,
And greed for money will breed bitterness
Between generations: men will cheat
Each other as they calmly counterfeit
Religious faith. The winter and the spring
Will pass mankind unmarked[26], no one will bring
The wine to celebrate such moments then;
Instead they'll spill the blood of fellow men.

It is a powerful picture of political and moral decay and the loss of old aristocratic values. The breaking down of class distinctions and the mixing of different races are all part of this destruction of traditional values. In contrast with the views of the Christians, there is no indication that the disasters of the Muslim conquest were part of God's punishment for sin. It was rather a disaster decreed by fate. It is, of course, put in the mouth of the general who knows that he will be defeated and killed and the order he is supporting will disappear, but it is hard to imagine that his bleak view of the effects of the coming of Muslim rule does not reflect the opinions of many of the Iranian aristocrats of the centuries which followed the conquests.

None of the other areas of the Muslim world remodelled its ancient history in this striking and original fashion or used it to articulate their adherence to pre-Islamic cultural values and their disdain for the uncouth bearers of the new revelation. It is true that some Syriac chroniclers traced the history of their church back to ancient times and the Coptic biographies of the Patriarchs of Alexandria were translated into Arabic. These works may have sustained the dwindling Christian populations of Syria and Egypt by proving the antiquity and steadfastness of their churches but they could hardly provide a national myth at a time when more and more Syrians and Egyptians were converting to Islam. The great strength of New Persian culture was that it could appeal to Muslim and non-Muslim Persians alike and provide a new basis for cultural identity, not tied to the coat-strings of a fading religion. It is from this largely secular, court background, not the writings of Zoroastrians priests that the culture emerges. Without the survival of a consciously Iranian aristocracy this would not have been possible. Among the Syrians and Copts, the only cultural leadership was supplied by the churches and monasteries and its appeal was not wide enough to generate cultural self-sufficiency.

The survival of ancient Iranian culture can also be seen in the architecture. The architecture of the Achaemenid period, with its tall stone columns and wooden roofed halls seems to have disappeared after the fall of the empire in the wake of Alexander's conquests. However, in the first centuries of the common era, a new style began to develop. This was marked by two distinct but frequently juxtaposed forms, the dome chamber and the *ivan*. The characteristic Persian dome chamber with the round dome supported by squinches over a square chamber can be seen in the palace of the first of the Sasanian *shah*s, Ardashir I at Firuzabad. Later examples can be seen at Sarvistan (if this is indeed a later Sasanian building). The *ivan* was the open arch, looking out on a courtyard, as could be seen in the spectacular Tāq-i Kisrā near Baghdad. The *ivan* and the dome chamber together formed the most typical architectural unit of Sasanian monumental building. We have very little evidence about the architectural forms of early mosques in Iran but it is clear that when we begin to find surviving examples of Islamic building in post-conquest Iran, like the shrine of the 12 Imams in Yazd or the Masjid-i Jom'eh in Isfahan they use the dome chamber and in Isfahan, the dome chamber and the *ivan* come together as they had done at Firuzabad and Sarvistan. The palace of the great Abbasid caliph al-Manṣūr at Baghdad was certainly characterised by a tall brick dome, a symbol of royalty derived directly from the Sasanian past. The old Persian empire was a source of magnificence and prestige among Muslim rulers, a clear physical manifestation of the continuing status and vitality of old Iranian norms.

Sasanian architecture also used new materials. In place of the finely cut stones and great wooden beams of Achaemenid architecture, it employs brick and rubble masonry, covered with carved and moulded stucco in the case of high-status building. The legacy of brick and plaster building survives into the Muslim period.

In important ways, Firdausi's lament for ancient glories brings us to the heart of the medieval and modern dilemmas of Iranianness, caught between the reverence for traditional Iranian values and the respect for Islamic norms. The old Sasanian *shah*s were the epitome of courtly virtues, stylish monarchy and political wisdom but they lacked the true religion. The Arabs by contrast were gross and dismal but, one had to admit, the bringers of the true faith. One is irresistibly reminded of the verdict of *1066 and All That* on the English civil war in which, you will remember, that the royalist cavaliers were wrong but romantic while the republican puritans were right but repulsive. The dilemma was strikingly brought home to me on a visit to Iran in the 1990s at the height of the austerity of the Islamic republic. At that time, because of the vagaries of the Muslim calendar, Ramadan, the holy month when Muslims fast from sunrise to sunset was in March. March is also, and always, the time of the great Persian New Year festival of Nauruz, a festival which has been celebrated without interruption since Achaemenid times. Ancient custom dictates that Iranian families should celebrate the thirteenth day of the New Year by spending the day picnicking in the countryside. I do not know how the pious addressed this conflict of interest but I can report from personal observation that the fields and meadows around Shiraz, bright with fresh grass and spring flowers, were replete with Persian families, enjoying their food in the broadest daylight untroubled by the strictures of the clerics. It represented the clearest triumph of those old Iranian values which demonstrated how they had survived the Arab-Islamic conquests.

Notes:

1. See Lazard 1975: 595-632.
2. There is a vast literature on the *Shāhnāma*. For Anglophone readers the best starting point is now in Davis 2007.
3. For a general history of these dynasties see Madelung, 1975: 198-249. For the best discussion of Tabaristan through the Arab conquest see Pourshariati 2008: 287-318. On their attachment to the pre-Islamic past as a sources of legitimacy see Bosworth 1973: 51-62.
4. Pourshariati 2008: 313-14.
5. Bosworth 1996: 178-180.
6. See Bosworth 1996 and Minorsky 1958.
7. Tabari 1867: 2650-2655.
8. Pourshariati 1998: 41-81 especially 62f.
9. See Morony 1984 for a full discussion of late Sasanian and early Islamic Iraq.
10. Baladhuri 1866: 265.
11. Baladhuri 1866: 271.
12. Jahshiyari 1938: 230-232.
13. Baladhuri 1866: 280.
14. The only exception to this is a recent study on Nabataean agriculture for which see now Hämeen-Anttila 2006. But as the title implies, it celebrates good farming rather than an elite cultural heritage.
15. For a recent discussion of large estate in late antiquity, especially in Egypt, see Sarris, 2004: 55-71.
16. On landholding in late Byzantine Egypt, see Hardy 1931 and Gascou 1985: 1-90. On the Apion estates, see Sarris 2006.
17. Bulliet 1979.
18. On the Barmakids see van Bladel, 'The Bactrian Background of the Barmakids' (*forthcoming*).
19. The Coptic revolts of ninth century Egypt seem to have been protests against brutal over-taxation but do not seem to have been accompanied by any calls to restore Christian rule.
20. On Sunbādh see Sadighi 1938: 133-134, 143-144.
21. Bosworth 1973: 57-58.
22. Jahshiyari 1938: 2-11.
23. See Davis 2004: 494-445.
24. Black was the court colour of the Abbasid Caliphs from 750 onwards.
25. Sasanian king who ruled 420-438 CE and who was considered the epitome of the courtly warrior, a great hunter and patron of musicians.
26. A reference to the great traditional Iranian feast of Nauruz, the New Year, which is celebrated in March on the spring equinox when seedlings begin to sprout.

3

The Persistent Older Heritage in the Medieval Iranian Lands

C. Edmund Bosworth
(University of Manchester, Emeritus)

When the last Sasanian emperor Yazdigird III was killed at Marv in 651 CE, the Arabs were in process of overrunning Iran as far as the Oxus and this process was largely completed a century later. In the northwest, Azerbaijan was mainly secured during ‘Uthmān's caliphate (644–656 CE), with Ardabil becoming its administrative centre; Darband or Bāb al-Abwāb on the western shore of the Caspian Sea was reached and was to form a base for attacks on the Khazars of the steppes north of the Caucasus. At the other end of the Iranian plateau, two-pronged attacks secured Sistan when in 651 CE ‘Uthmān's commander al-Rabī‘ b. Ziyād al-Ḥārithī made peace with the notables, civil and religious, of Zarang, and then, Arab raiders, proceeding by the route across the Great Desert and Tabas (at this time the preferred route to Khorasan rather than the more northerly one along the southern rim of the Elburz chain), secured Khorasan. The Arabs made the Marv oasis their concentration-point in Khorasan, with considerable settlement there (it was not till the time of the Tahirids that Nishapur rose to prominence as the administrative centre of the province), and from there penetrated to Balkh and Tukharistan in what is now northern Afghanistan, and then across the Oxus into Sogdia.[1] Only the Elburz mountain region and the Caspian coastlands remained substantially free of Arab control, inimical as they were to the desert Arabs in habitat and climate (as some Arabic verses put it, ‘Jurjān! What has made you know what Jurjān is! — A mouthful of figs and speedy death! — When a carpenter sees a Khorasani, he makes for him a funeral bier according to his size!’).[2]

During the eighth century CE, Iran was in process of becoming Muslim, even if the Islam in question contained many heterodox elements. Moreover, from this century onwards we have documentary evidence for the emergence of a New Persian language which, its vocabulary swollen by an influx of Arab vocabulary and Arabisms and probably influenced also by other languages to the north and east of Persia proper, was a vigorous and flexible new language and not just a simple continuation of Middle Persian.[3] The future for Iran was with an Islam-based religious ethos and culture. Nevertheless, breaks with the past are often far from cataclysmic, and this was certainly the case with Iran in medieval Islamic times. In the administration and court culture of the Umayyad and Abbasid caliphs, the first rulers installed at Damascus and the second ones in Iraq, what had been an integral part of the Sasanian empire, influences from the superior civilisation of Iran are discernible at an early date. If the office of the chief executive officer or vizier, as it evolved in early Abbasid times, was essentially an Arab and not an Iranian institution,[4] the network of administrative and financial departments, the *dīwāns*, had clear links with the Iranian past. These organs of government continued to be run, certainly in Iraq and Iran, by Persian secretaries; until the *naql al-dīwān* decreed by ʻAbd al-Malik in c. 697 CE, records of govermental transactions in Iraq and western Iran continued to be written in Persian language, and in the eastern provinces like Khorasan the change to Arabic was not made until 742 CE.[5] A characteristic institution of the medieval caliphate and then its successor states, the state postal and intelligence service, the *barīd,* has roots in both the Byzantine and Sasanian empires; it was obviously necessary for the ruler to be able to exert some form of control over distant provinces whose governors were prone to hold back the central government's share of taxation collected or even to rebel.[6] The sinologist Karl Wittfogel regarded such a communications network as the necessary concomitant of what he called ‘hydraulic societies’, inevitably despotic and centralising ones, because the upkeep and management of complex irrigation systems in lands like Mesopotamia, the Iranian oasis cities and the valley of the Zarafshan river in Sogdia was only possible with central government control and investment.[7]

Examples like these could be multiplied. They were part of a symbiosis of two separate cultural traditions, the Arab-Islamic one and the Iranian one, a symbiosis largely achieved by the ninth century. This was not, however, reached without tensions and difficulties. The religious scholars, *ʻulamā'* and *fuqahā'*, with attitudes rooted in the places where Islam as a religion and law had evolved — Medina, Mecca, Damascus and the Iraqi garrison cities — were suspicious of Persian influences associated, in their minds, with material luxury and opulent living and with heterodox religious influences such as Zoroastrianism, Nestorian Christianity, Mazdakism and Manicheism.

For their part, the Persians could point to the glories of their historical past, with extant monuments like the Tāq-i Kisrā at Ctesiphon, the ruins of Persepolis, the Achaemenid and Sasanian-period rock reliefs and the network of fire temples which still survived in the Persian lands up to four centuries after Prophet Muhammad's mission. A recollection of such glories and of a superior material culture in general formed part of the arguments of the Persian proponents of the Shuʻūbiyya in the ninth century, the assertion that Muhammad's mission and the faith he brought was not a uniquely Arab phenomenon but one for all the Qur'anic *shuʻūb*, peoples and races. H.A.R. Gibb's conclusion, after a consideration of the sociological as well as the literary aspect of the Shuʻūbiyya controversies, was that the Arabs' defensive reaction was largely successful,[8] but this seems exaggerated (Gibb was in general unsympathetic to the Persian contribution to Islam and not particularly knowledgeable about it). The partisans of the 'Ajamīs were successful in that the resultant Islamic civilisation of the central and eastern lands, from the Levant to Central Asia and what was to become Muslim India, became in many regards an amalgam of the two traditions, a coming together on equal terms, and not just an absorption by the Arab Muslim tradition of those Persian elements which it chose consciously to accept whilst rejecting others.[9]

As the overarching authority of the Iraq-based caliphate waned during the course of the ninth century, various lines of provincial governors and military commanders who had been sent to secure frontier regions, emerged as being increasingly autonomous in practice, however meticulous they might be in observing the external signs of dependence. The Abbasids continued to be acknowledged in the Friday *khuṭba* or bidding prayer and on the *sikka*, the gold and silver coinage where the caliph's name would appear first, and tribute, often in the form of slaves captured in war or purchased from the South Russian steppes and on the frontiers of the Persian lands beyond the Oxus, Central Asia, continued to be forwarded to Baghdad and Samarra. It happened that, in several cases, as with the Yazīdī Shīrwān-Shāhs in the eastern Caucasus region, various Daylamī and Kurdish petty princes in Azerbaijan, and the Samanids in Transoxania and then in Khorasan, much of the reality of the fiction of caliphally-delegated authority fell away, with tribute and presents ceasing to be sent to the caliphs. A more decisive reaction against even a watered-down caliphal authority is seen in the case of the Saffarids, who from a base in Sistan built up a mighty if ephemeral military empire in the southern and eastern Persian lands as far as the fringes of India, and who, having carved out their empire by their own hands, expressly rejected any link with the Abbasids when it suited them and often spoke of them with contempt. In the Caspian provinces, there long persisted princely lines whose genealogies seem genuinely to have been traceable back to Sasanian times, and older traditions long continued there, including use of the Pahlavi form of Middle Persian for lapidary and monumental, and perhaps for chancery, purposes. As late as the early eleventh century, the Bawandid Ispahbads of Tabaristan (who traced their descent either to one Baw, grandson of Kawus, son of the Sasanian emperor Kawad, who had been Ispahbad of the province for the Khusrau Aparwiz, or to a Zoroastrian priest of Ray) were placing legends in Pahlavi as well as Arabic on two tomb towers they erected in Tabaristan/Mazandaran.[10] Islamic religion was not firmly established there till the coming of Zaydī Shi'ism to Daylam, Gilan and Tabaristan in the later ninth and tenth centuries, as promoted by the two Ḥasanid *dā'ī*s or propagandists from Ray, al-Ḥasan and Muhammad b. Zayd, and then by the Ḥusaynid al-Ḥasan b. 'Alī al-Uṭrūsh. These Zaydiyya were obviously upholders of the claims of the House of 'Alī, and not of the Abbasids, as the true caliph-imams, and may be accounted as continuing the heterodox traditions characteristic of these regions, albeit now in an Islamic form.[11]

In addition to such older lines, new, increasingly, increasingly autonomous or even independent ones were thus evolving, but none of these last felt able to repudiate the past. For their authority depended not only on the sword, sheer military force, but on a sense, felt in varying degrees, that the recovery of or the forging of links with the past was necessary for the firmness of their authority over the lands they ruled. Across the whole Islamic world, from West Africa to Indonesia, rulers have at various times sought to establish connections with the lineage of the Prophet Muhammad himself or at least, with the Arab people, the divinely-chosen race from whose midst the Prophet had arisen. This is what the Tahirid governors of Khorasan and the East attempted to do during the middle decades of the ninth century. The family was undoubtedly Persian, from the region of Herat and Pushang in what is now western Afghanistan. The first known member of the family was a *mawlā* or client of one of the governors of Sistan for the early Umayyads, Ṭalḥa b. ʻAbdallāh al-Khuzāʼī, and through this, subsequent Tahirids claimed affiliation to the Arab tribe of Khuzāʻa, in some respects considered more noble than the Prophet's own tribe of Quraysh in Mecca. Although the connection was in the ninth century satirised by a disgruntled Arab poet genuinely from Khuzāʻa, Diʻbil b. ʻAlī, by a curious reversal of events the tribe now came to derive glory from the Tahirid connection and the latter line's humble origins in *walāʼ* or clientage, whilst at the same time one of their eulogists gave ʻAbdallāh b. Ṭāhir (d. 845) a noble Persian origin by attaching him to Rustam; these early Tahirids were obviously happy to accept the best of both worlds. A later member of the family, ʻUbaydallāh b. ʻAbdallāh b. Ṭāhir (d. 913), governor of Baghdad and a noted littérateur and patron of scholars, became acknowledged as ʻShaykh of Khuzāʻaʼ, head of the tribe; it seems that, with the family's power now based in Baghdad in the second half of the ninth century, its Persian origins were now conveniently downplayed or even forgotten.[12]

The Tahirids' Arab connection was undeniably authentic, but the connections with the Arab past later claimed by some other Persian ruling dynasties were far-fetched, with the prestige of an attachment to the Prophet Muhammad and his house leading some of their apologists and eulogists to ludicrous lengths. The opening years of the tenth century usher in what Minorsky called ʻthe Daylamī interlude of Persian history,ʼ when hitherto obscure and submerged elements within the Persian lands, so far as we can tell only imperfectly Islamised, burst forth from northwestern Persia and the western Elburz mountain chain region.[13] The catalyst for this historical process is far from clear, but Daylamīs, Jīlīs and Kurds now established their authority over almost the whole of the Persian plateau except for Khorasan. The most vigorous and successful family here were the Buyids, the three founding Buyid brothers from Daylam being originally mercenaries in the armies of the caliphs in western Persia. By the middle of the tenth century the Buyid tribal confederation extended over not only, as remarked, much of Persia proper but also much of Iraq, with the Abbasid caliphate, now at its lowest ebb for practical political and military power, under the Buyids' tutelage. The greatest of the Buyid Amirs, 'Aḍud al-Dawla Fanā-Khusrau (r. 949–982), by the end of his reign controlled territories from the Jazira, northern Mesopotamia, to Kerman in southeastern Persia.[14] Although only of the second generation of Buyid princes, 'Aḍud al-Dawla, and subsequently his successors, speedily integrated themselves almost wholly into the fabric of Arab-Islamic culture. 'Aḍud al-Dawla and his brother-rulers employed viziers who were some of the outstanding scholars, poets and exponents in general of *adab*, of what was a particularly glorious age culturally, the century which the Swiss orientalist Adam Mez characterised as the Renaissance of Islam. 'Aḍud al-Dawla was a noted patron of Arabic culture (see further below) and the greatest of Arab poets of the time, al-Mutanabbī, spent some of the happier and more fruitful months of his distinctly *mouvementée* career at his court in Shiraz in 965 CE, with the six *'Aḍudiyyāt* which he wrote there amongst the finest of his *qaṣīda*s or odes.[15]

Hence it was already in just this second generation of Buyid rule that a eulogist should arise with the aim of showing that the Buyids were no longer crude barbarians from the backwoods of northwestern Persia but had become part of the community of civilised Muslims. A member of the famed Ṣābi' family of scientists and scholars, originally from a classical pagan background at Harran in northern Syria, Abū Isḥāq Ibrāḥīm (d. 994), composed in Arabic for 'Aḍud al-Dawla a laudatory history of the Buyids, the *Kitāb al-Tāj fī akhbār al-dawla al-daylamiyya,* now only fragmentarily known. The work was clearly intended to to vaunt the reputation of the Daylamīs in general and also to extol the personal power of 'Aḍud al-Dawla wa-Tāj al-Milla, the latter *laqab* or honorific of 'Crown of the Religious Community', acquired from the caliph towards the end of his life, being particularly dear to him as referring to one of the actual appurtenances of royalty in the Persian tradition, the crown.[16] Al-Ṣābi' repeats a story that appears in other Arab sources of the tenth century, hence must have had a certain currency in its time,[17] that in distant times the Buyid brothers had not been ethnically Daylami and Persian at all, but had stemmed from a part of the Yemeni tribe of Ḍabba that had migrated as a result of tribal warfare within the Arabian peninsula to Daylam, merged with the surrounding population, lost their Arabic language but retained the Arab virtues of hospitality and liberality and their military prowess.[18] Some decades later, Ibn Ḥassūl, an official of the early Seljuqs — hence in the service of a rising power hostile to the Buyids — in a eulogy of the Turkish ethnicity of his masters poured scorn on the claim of al-Ṣābi'. He pointed out that there was no historical record of a migration of the Banū Ḍabba and that the Buyids' eulogist had deliberately chosen as the protagonists of his tale a tribe with a notoriously confused genealogy; sarcastically, he added that if al-Ṣābi' had been able, he would have attached 'Aḍud al-Dawla to the Prophet's tribe of Quraysh.[19]

Yet 'Aḍud al-Dawla is a figure who spans both the Persian and the Arab ethnic and cultural aspects of the Perso-Islamic civilisation of the time. He presumably enjoyed being lauded by al-Ṣābi', since it was he who expressly commissioned the work. On the other hand, he was clearly aware of his family's real origins and of the glorious past of the Persian lands that he ruled. It has been suggested by Wilferd Madelung that ideas of a restoration of the ancient Persian kingship were current amongst the Daylamīs and Jīlīs at the time of the rise to power of the Buyid brothers out of the entourage of the Daylamī *condottiere* Mardāwīj b. Ziyār, progenitor of the Ziyarid line which was to rule in Tabaristan and Gorgan until almost the end of the eleventh century. Mardāwīj's original master, the Jīliī Asfār b. Shīrūya had at one point used much violence against the Muslims of Qazwin before Mardāwīj, now his rival for power in northern Persia, turned on him and killed him in c. 931 CE. Arabic historians like al-Mas'ūdī, Miskawayh and Ibn al-Athīr record that Mardāwīj was hostile towards at least official Islamic religion, allowing his troops at Dinawar and Hamadan to massacre members of the Muslim religious classes, *'ulamā'* and Sufis alike, and had ambitions of restoring the old Persian empire before he was murdered by his own Turkish *ghulāms* in 935 CE; such orthodox Muslim historians were, of course, themselves inevitably hostile to figures like Asfār and Mardāwīj, and one should perhaps not take everything they write *au pied de la lettre*. They go on to record that, in addition to the ancient Persian New Year festival of Nauruz (which many earlier Islamic rulers, including the Abbasid caliphs themselves already observed), Mardāwīj celebrated the ancient festivals of Mihrgan and Sadeh (as were the Buyids and the strictly Sunni orthodox Ghaznavids after him to do). He had a golden throne made for himself; he studied the ways of the emperors before adopting the tunic (*badana*) they had worn, and he had fashioned for his head a bejewelled, gold crown (*tāj*) on the pattern of Khusrau Anushirwan's. Plannning just before his death to march on Baghdad from his base in Ahwaz, he gave instructions for the *īwān Kisrā*, the palace of the Khusrau at Ctesiphon or al-Madā'in, to be restored as his future residence in Iraq.[20]

A possible manifestation of this nostalgia for the ancient Persian past current at this time amongst certain circles of the Daylamīs and Jīlīs was the Buyids' adoption of the title *shāhānshāh* 'king of kings,' implying a claim to supreme kingship independent of the caliphs in Iraq and of any theoretical act of delegation by them.[21] The title is particularly associated with 'Aḍud al-Dawla, but seems to have been tentatively adopted by his predecessor and father Rukn al-Dawla Ḥasan b. Būya, and actually used by 'Aḍud al-Dawla during his father's lifetime. The whole question of 'Aḍud al-Dawla's titulature and the interplay of the Arab-Muslim names and titles and the nationalist Persian ones, has been discussed in detail by Professor Richter-Bernburg against a background of the Amir's steady acquisition of power across a vast swathe of the Middle East and his relations with the 'Abbasid caliphs.[22] G.C. Miles described a silver portrait medallion minted at al-Muḥammadiyya / Ray by Rukn al-Dawla in 962 CE/AH 351 which portrays the ruler wearing a crown with a Pahlavi inscription referring to him as *shāhānhshāh*, and a further gold commemorative medallion from the year 970 CE/AH 359 depicts him in the fashion of the Sasanian emperors, with a Pahlavi legend containing traditional formulae of invocation for the Persian monarchs, *farrah afzūd Shāhān Shāh* and *dīr zīy Shā /Pan(n)ā Khusrau.*[23]

'Aḍud al-Dawla is described in the extant fragment of Abū Isḥāq al-Ṣābi''s *Kitāb al-Tāj* as *Mawlānā al-Malik Shāhānshāh*, and he started using the title on his coins soon after he had in 976 CE/AH 366 conquered Iraq, entering Baghdad in the next year and now reigning over the united Buyid lands south of Ray and Jibāl; coins with the title *Shāhānshāh* are extant from 981 CE/AH 370 till his death two years later.[24] The Buyids of the second generation favoured Persian personal names, like Fanā-Khusrau, Shīrzīl, Bakhtiyār and Fīrūz, whereas the previous generation of the three sons of their progenitor Būya, himself almost certainly a very recent entrant to the Islamic faith, are found with the typical Muslim ones of the type that one might expect of the sons of a convert, 'Alī, Ḥasan and Aḥmad. The *Kitāb al-Tāj* was apparently also used, it seems for the first time expressly in literature, to give expression to the Buyids' claim to descent from the Sasanian emperor Bahram Gur (the great Khwarazmian scholar Abū Rayḥān al-Bīrūnī, however, considered that claims of an Arab and a Sasanian Persian genealogy for the Buyids were equally spurious).[25]

Al-Mutanabbī had already addressed 'Aḍud al-Dawla in his odes with the exalted titles of *Shāhānshāh* and *Malik al-mulūk*,[26] and in his later years the Amir was particularly insistent that the correct protocol, including the designation Shāhānshāh, should be used in addressing him. A messenger sent by him to Baghdad in 977 CE instructed the reluctant caliph al-Ṭā'i' to come out and meet him ceremonially, following the traditional practice of *istiqbāl*, by telling him that the Buyid Amir was an outstanding king, in the rank of the exalted Khusraus (*jārī majāriya'l-akāsira al-mu'aẓẓamīn*). The investiture in the caliph's palace of the Amir was that of an Islamic ruler, as the sophisticated and learned 'Aḍud al-Dawla genuinely was, a ruler who acknowledged the moral and spiritual authority of the caliph, God's shadow on earth, with *baraka* graciously delegated to him by the Abbasid through this ceremony. But it was also that of a traditional, Persian-type monarch, exercising practical power by force of his personality and military might, who intended to act as the caliph's partner in something like an imperial structure. This dual arrangement was to be sealed by the marriage of one of his daughters with al-Ṭā'i'; the historian of the Buyids, Miskawayh, expressly states that the Amir's hope was for a son from this union who would succeed to the caliphate and unite in himself both Abbasid and Buyid lineage. The marriage took place all right in 980 CE, but the canny caliph took care never to consummate it, on grounds of the girl's youth, so that no child was ever born of the projected union.[27]

'Aḍud al-Dawla and other Buyids of his and the following generations were highly civilised rulers, literate in Arabic; 'Aḍud al-Dawla was himself an Arabic speaker, who addressed the caliph in Arabic when he received from him his honorific title of Tāj al-Milla, and some Arabic verses by him and by others of the family are given by al-Tha'ālibī [28]. They were patrons of a dazzling array of poets, stylists, philosophers and scientists at the various provincial courts of western and outhern Persia and Iraq, including such great names as the Ṣāḥib Ismā'īl b. 'Abbād, Abu 'l-Faḍl Ibn al-'Amīd, al-Muhallabī, Abū Ḥayyān al-Tawḥīdī, Ibn Baqiyya and many others.[29] One should not take the Buyids' interest in the older Persian heritage, as just outlined, as envisaging any abandonment of the basically Islamic nature of their power and authority. It is true that, quite early in his reign, in 955 CE, when he was ruling the province of Fars only, on his return from campaigning at Isfahan, 'Aḍud al-Dawla visited the ruins of Persepolis. Whether he had a conscious motive of imbibing something of the aura of the glories of the Achaemenids is not known, although he commissioned a Kufic-script Arabic inscription recording the visit of the Amir Fanā-Khusrau and had it placed on the doorway into Darius the Great's palace next to two Pahlavi inscriptions of the early Sasanian ruler Shapur II (310–379 CE). A second inscription of his mentions that a Zoroastrian *mōbad* from Kazerun, one Marasfand, translated Pahlavi inscriptions for the Amir, whilst another person, 'Alī b. al-Sarī al-Karajī, from his name clearly a Muslim, probably wrote down the Arabic translation.[30] The Amir's recording of his visit must have been meant as a proclamation for the wider Muslim public of the time, and there is nothing in the inscriptions implying that 'Aḍud al-Dawla thought of himself as a descendant of the Sasanians or in any way an heir to them. Indeed, we know that he performed the religious duties prescribed by Islam with great fidelity, and showed his devotion to Shi'ism by building works at the shrines of 'Alī at Najaf and al-Ḥusayn b. 'Alī at Karbala.[31]

If he aimed at an Islamised form of ancient Persian kingship, 'Aḍud al-Dawla did not succeed, and his less forceful successors were no more successful. His son Bahā' al-Dawla retained the designation Shāhānshāh in his titulature and on his coins, as did his kinsman in Ray, Fakhr al-Dawla 'Alī's son Majd al-Dawla Rustam, but whereas 'Aḍud al-Dawla had assumed the title Shāhānshāh unilaterally and without reference to Baghdad, by the eleventh century the title had become one bestowed by the Abbasid caliph as part of the array of honorifics customarily granted by him to secular rulers on their accession. For a contemporary historian like the Ghaznavid one Abu 'l-Faḍl Bayhaqī, the title was so characteristic of the Buyids that he refers to them in his *History of Sultan Mas'ūd* as the *Shāhānshāhiyān*.[32] After Bahā' al-Dawla's death in 1012, there were undignified and acrimonious disputes on various occasions between his sons Sulṭān al-Dawla, Jalāl al-Dawla and Musharrif al-Dawla in southern Persia and Iraq, and with Majd al-Dawla Rustam in Ray also involved, over assumption of the title. In the 1030s, the caliph al-Qā'im was drawn in when the rivals Jalāl al-Dawla and his nephew 'Imād al-Dīn Abū Kālījār both claimed the title and applied to al-Qā'im for it. It is well known that when Jalāl al-Dawla's new titles were read out in the *khuṭba* at Baghdad in 1038, there were protests from both popular and religious elements against a designation abhorrent to Islamic orthodoxy, for which only God was King of Kings, but the majority opinion of the *'ulamā'* thereupon consulted was that it was licit. The caliphs' thereby-acquired right to grant such a title established their claim of ultimate moral power and superiority within the Islamic polity.[33]

The Samanids, rather older contemporaries of the early Buyids, succeeded to much of the Tahirid heritage in the eastern Islamic lands. They were of Persian *dehqān* origin, from the Oxus valley lands, apparently from the Balkh and Tukharistan region; in the first part of the eighth century, Sāmān-Khudā, the first historically attested member of the line, became a Muslim and served one of the last Umayyad governors of Khorasan. It was thus less easy for the Samanids to claim any links with the Arab-Islamic past than for the Tahirids, and there is no information suggesting that they ever tried to do this, although their courts in Transoxania and Khorasan became in the tenth century brilliant centres of Arabic learning, where, encouraged by the Amirs and their ministers, literature and science flourished, as the extensive sections on the poets of those two provinces in part four of al-Tha'ālibī's literary anthology, the *Yatīmat al-dahr*, show.[34] But these regions were also, as is well-known, of vital importance in the renaissance of New Persian language and literature, and the aristocratic Persian ethnic origins of the Amirs remained to the fore. Al-Bīrūnī had no connection with the Buyids and no debt of gratitude to them, hence could afford to dismiss claims by the Buyids' apologists giving them a glorious past. He had, however, to concede the claims of the line of his own patron Shams al-Ma'ālī Qābūs b. Wushmagīr, the ruler of Gorgan and Tabaristan and nephew of Mardāwīj's brother, the dynasty of the Ziyarids: that Mardāwīj had a dual exalted descent, from a noble house of Gilan and, much more splendidly, from the Sasanian emperor Kawad.[35]

As for the Samanids, al-Bīrūnī's first patron when he left Khwarazm was one of the last Samanid Amirs, Manṣūr b. Nūḥ II (999 CE/AH 387–389), and he states, followed by later historians recording historical events in Khorasan and the east like Ibn al-Athīr, that the Samanids were 'incontestably' (*lā yukhālif aḥad*) from the descent of the father of Bahram Chubin, Bahram Gushnasp.[36] This line was of the noble family of Mihran, one of the seven great houses of Sasanian Persia, hereditary Ispahbads of Ray and northern Persia. The Mihranids actually claimed descent from the Sasanians' predecessors, the Parthian Arsacids, a pretension which Bahram Chubin had used for his revolt in 590 CE against the emperor Hormizd IV and his temporary occupation of the imperial throne for one year as Bahram VI. Although Bahram had to flee across the Oxus and enter the service of the Khāqān of the Turks and was soon afterwards assassinated, his adventurous career made a deep impression on the Persian national consciousness and gave rise to a popular romance in Pahlavi, utilised by later Islamic historical and *adab* sources, and by Firdausi for the *Shāhnāmah*.[37] An interesting point recently brought to light by Luke Treadwell is that the Amir Manṣūr b. Nūḥ I (976 CE/AH 350–365), during the middle years of his reign minted at Bukhara a silver medallion very similar to Rukn al-Dawla's one of 962 CE/AH 352 and with the title *Shāhānshāh* on it though without the monarch's portrait. He thinks that this issue, so far as is known an isolated one, could have been a conscious reply to Buyid claims by the Samanid, who through much of his reign was at odds with Rukn al-Dawla over control of Ray and its region.[38]

Lesser princely families of both the northeastern and northwestern extremities of the Persian world were equally attracted by the prospect of attaching themselves to the heroic Persian past. The anonymous Persian geography, written in 982 CE in Guzgan, what is now northwestern Afghanistan, for the local line of Farighunid amirs (perhaps even composed by a member of the family), the *Ḥudūd al-ʿālam* or 'Limits of the World,' states that the Farighunids were descended from the mythical hero Āfridhūn / Farīdūn.[39] The Yazīdī Shīrwān-Shāhs of eastern Transcaucasia were undoubtedly of Qaysī or North Arab origin. The founder, Yazīd b. Mazyad al-Shaybānī, was governor of this region and of Armenia, Arran and Azerbaijan for the early Abbasid caliphs, and he founded a line which was to be unusually long-lasting, certainly till the time of Timur and possibly till that of the Safavids. We do not know whether they made any claims to an ancient, distinguished lineage, but what is interesting is that this Arab family, now firmly fixed in a Persian, Kurdish and Caucasian milieu, intermarrying with local Caucasian families and completely isolated from the heartland of Arab-Islamic culture, within two centuries had clearly become Persianised in outlook, judging by the fact that after c. 1000 CE, the Shāhs adopted Persian regnal names typical of the Persian mythical past, such as Manuchihr, Faridun, Garshasp, Kay Qubad, etc.; later historians like the Mongol-period one Rashīd al-Dīn and the Ottoman one Münejjim-Bashï assumed as a matter of course that the Shāhs were Persians of Sasanian descent.[40]

That someone like Samān-Khudā should be descended from the Mihranids must have seemed to contemporaries perfectly possible, given the power and renown of his descendants, the Samanid dynasty, and perhaps indeed they were so descended; but claims made by obsequious eulogists for their sister dynasty of the Saffarids of Sistan must have been harder to swallow. They do, however, demonstrate how strong the search to find roots in the past could be for the most unlikely of subjects. The Saffarids arose from a military adventurer in Zarang, the capital of Sistan, in the mid-ninth century, Yaʿqūb b. Layth. The origins of Yaʿqūb and his brother and successor ʿAmr were undoubtedly humble — they had been respectively a coppersmith and a stonemason or mule hirer — but the two brothers built up, by force of arms and sheer *élan*, a mighty if transient military empire which in the second half of the ninth century stretched from the region of Kabul in the east to the fringes of Iraq in the west, and from Oman across the Persian Gulf in the south to the Oxus river in the north. According to the local history of the province, the *Tārīkh-i Sīstān*, which not surprisingly lauds the achievements of the Saffarids as local boys who had made good in a spectacular way, Yaʿqūb would openly boast of his lowly origins and proclaim that his achievement stemmed entirely from his own strong arm and not from any inherited prestige or family *baraka*. He regarded the Abbasid caliphs with contempt and thought that their power was based on fraud and deceit.[41]

Hence it is not surprising that Ya'qūb had no use for Arabic learning. It is said that when, after his conquest of Herat and Pushang from the Tahirids in 867 CE, poets attached themselves to him and praised him and his victories in Arabic, Ya'qūb angrily expostulated that their verses were unintelligible to him, and he got his chief secretary, one Muhammad b. Waṣīf, to eulogise him in New Persian; the 23 verses that have been preserved from these, dating from around the 860s, rank as one of the earliest monuments of Islamic New Persian literature.[42] These verses do not contain any references relevant to our present purpose, but the *Tārīkh-i Sīstān*, in many ways a dynastic history of the Saffarids, attributes to Ya'qūb a lengthy Persian genealogy not only going back to Khusrau Aparwiz, Kawad, Shapur, Ardashir and Sasan, but even further to mythical heroes like Faridun, Jamshid and the first man Kayumarth.[43] One might take this lineage as having been fabricated by the unknown author of the main part of the *History*, who seems to have written in the second half of the eleventh century, in order to glorify the Saffarids when they had settled down in comparative peace and in a diminished role as Amirs of Sistan only, and when the last ruler of the line, Khalaf b. Aḥmad, had achieved a great contemporary reputation within the Islamic world as a learned and cultured scholar. Khalaf presided over scholarly sessions, *majālis*, where questions of political science and philosophy were discussed, and is said to have commissioned a team of scholars to produce a 100-volume encyclopaedia of the Qur'anic sciences, expending on the project 20,000 *dinar*s; if it was ever completed, it has not surprisingly failed to survive.[44] Yet there remains evidence of claims made for the first Saffarids which is undoubtedly contemporary with Ya'qūb himself, a fragment of Arabic verse by a poet of Isfahan who apparently had strongly Shu'ūbī feelings although he had been a member of the Abbasid court circle in Iraq, one Abū Isḥāq Ibrāhīm b. Mamshādh. It is cited in a later literary source, that of Yāqūt in his work of literary biography, the *Irshād al-arīb*, and was brought to prominence by the late Samuel Stern. In it, the words are put into the Saffarid Amir's mouth that he is the descendant of the hero Jam; that he holds the *'alam al-kābiyān*, banner of the blacksmith Kaveh, the ancient symbol of Persian royal authority, captured by the Arabs from the Sasanians at the battle of Qādisiyya in the mid-630s CE; and that he plans a career of conquest that will humiliate and uproot the Abbasids and revive the ancient empire of the Persian kings.[45] Whether Ya'qūb ever held such thoughts, or whether he even heard it recited (and he would not have understood the Arabic anyway) is, of course, wholly unknown; but it seems reasonable to assume that the poet's words, however full of typical persiflage, must have been not unpleasing to knowledgeable Saffarid circles when they learn about the poem.[46]

One could carry this study further and look at the survival of Persian cultural traditions in later ages under the mainly Turkish rulers of the Persian lands (panegyrists of the early Ghaznavids managed to attach the founder of the dynasty, Sebüktegin, whom we know was a Turkish military slave from Barskhan on the shores of the Issik Kol in what is now the Kyrgyz Republic, to the Sasanians through the fiction that a daughter of Yazdigird III had fled to the Turkish steppes and married a chief there[47] and even in Muslim India, but it is hoped that enough has been shown of the persistence and strength of the Persian heritage within the overarching fabric of Islamic society in the East during its first four centuries.

Notes:

1. Wellhausen 1927: 397ff.; Bosworth 1968: 13-14; Shaban 1970: 16ff. Zarrīnkūb 1975:18-28; Bosworth 1986.
2. al-Tha'ālibi1968: 130-131; Bayhaqī 1971: 580 (verses extemporised by the author himself whilst accompanying Sultan Mas'ūd on his expedition to Gorgan in 1035).
3. Emphasised by Utas 2006: 241-251. I am grateful to Professor Josef Elfenbein for a copy of this; cf. also Lazard 1975: 595-98, 606-611.
4. Sourdel (1959–60): 40-61; Goitein 1968: 168-196.
5. Sprengling 1939: 175-224, 325-36; *idem* 1940: 302-305.
6. Bosworth 1982a; Silverstein 2007: 53-140.
7. Wittfogel 1957.
8. Gibb 1953: 105-14; cf. Mottahedeh 1976: 161-182.
9. See in general Bosworth 1973: 51-62, repr. in *idem* 1977.
10. Madelung, 1982: 749-752 ; Blair, 1992: 85-90.
11. Madelung 1975: 206-212.
12. Bosworth 1969: 47-54, 71, repr. in *idem* 1982b; also *idem* 1975: 91-92, 104.
13. Minorsky 1932, repr. in *idem* 1964: 12-30.
14. See on him in general Bürgel 1965: 7-25; H. Busse 1975: 274-289; Kraemer 1986a: 272-285; Bürgel and Mottahedeh 1982.
15. For this period towards the close of his life (he was killed in 965 by Bedouin brigands on his way back from the Buyid capital Shiraz to Baghdad), see Blachère 1935: 243-244.
16. See on this author and the circumstances in which he composed his history Madelung 1967: 17-21.
17. The claim appears especially in the Arabic geographers of the tenth century; see Madelung 1969: 24 and n. 38.
18. *Ibid.* 20.
19. al-'Azzāwī 1940; cf. Bosworth 1973: 54, 57; and Bürgel 1965: 24 and n. 2.
20. Madelung1969: 86-89; Bosworth 1990; *idem*, 1982c:.
21. Madelung 1969: 92-93 further suggests that the adoption of this exalted title would have impressed tribal chiefs amongst the Daylamī and Jīlī soldiery who regarded the Buyid brothers as low-born upstarts.
22. Richter-Bernburg 1980: 83-102.
23. Treadwell 2003: 327-328, 336 n. 38. In the latter note, Treadwell makes the point that the second of these medallions has in the past been wrongly attributed to the son 'Aḍud al-Dawla and not to the father.
24. Richter-Bernburg 1980: 93; Treadwell 2003: 336 n. 38.
25. Madelung 1967: 24; al-Bīrūnī, tr. Sachau 1879: 45-46, who quotes al-Ṣābī for the genealogy.
26. Richter-Bernburg 1980: 91, 93, noting that 'Aḍud al-Dawla himself never used the Arabic form *Malik al-mulūk*, which the pious, however favourably inclined to the Amir, would have regarded as blasphemous; its Persian equivalent was apparently saved from this condemnation by its foreignness to Arab-Islamic religious feelings and by its connection with the Persian historical past.
27. Bürgel 1965: 24 and n. 2; Richter-Bernburg 1980: 93-94; Kraemer 1986a: 274-275.
28. al-Tha'ālibī, ed. 'Abd al-Ḥamīd 1956-58, II: 216-223.
29. See Kraemer 1986a: 103-272, and for the philosophers and scientists who worked under the aegis and patronage of the Buyids, *idem* 1986b: 30ff.
30. Richter-Bernburg 1980: 87; Blair 1992: 32-35.

31. Bürgel 1965: 23; Kraemer 1986a: 280.
32. Bayhaqī, ed. Fayyāḍ 1971: 44.
33. Amedroz 1905: 393-399; Madelung 1969: 171-183. It may, however, be observed that the title was not always obnoxious to the pious. In the early Persian translation of Abul-Qāsim Isḥāq al-Samarqandī's pioneering handbook of Hanafi law according to the Maturidi system of *kalām*, *al-Sawād al-a'ẓam*, the Imām Abū Ḥanīfa is described as the *kadkhudā-yi dīn va shāhānshāh-i fiqh* (I owe this reference to Mr Mohsen Ashtiany).
34. al-Tha'ālibī, ed. 'Abd al-Hamid 1956–58, IV: 64-193, 256-454.
35. al-Bīrūnī, tr. Sachau 1879: 47-48; cf. Bosworth 1973: 58.
36. *Ibid.* 48. However, the early Ghaznavid historian Gardīzī, in the section of his *Kitāb Zayn al-akhbār* devoted to the rulers of Khorasan, gives a much longer genealogy for the Samanids, one going back some fifty generations through legendary heroes like Hūshang to the first man, Kayūmarth. See Gardīzī, ed. Ḥabībī 1968: 145-146.
37. Bosworth 1973: 58-57; Shahbazi 1989.
38. Treadwell 2003: 328-330.
39. Minorsky 1937: 106.
40. Minorsky 1958: 134; Bosworth 1994: 60.
41. Bosworth 1994: 12-13, 168-169. However, Deborah Tor in her thought-provoking, revisionist, recent book suggests that Ya'qūb's detestation of the 'Abbasids was based less on a generalised view of the illegitimacy of their rule than on specific acts of treachery and deceit on the part of the caliph's brother al-Muwaffaq which had inveigled him into his unsuccessful campaign of 875 CE against Baghdad. See Tor 2007: 165ff.
42. Lazard 1964; Bosworth 1994: 174-177.
43. *Ibid.* 179-180.
44. Kraemer 1986b: 8-22.
45. Stern 1970: 535-555; Bosworth 1994: 177-180.
46. Again, Tor 2007: 169-172 is sceptical about the value of this poem as an appeal to nostalgia in Saffarid circles for the ancient Persian past and its glories, and even suggests that it was perhaps a piece of deliberate disinformation on the part of the Abbasids meant to discredit Ya'qūb. This is necessarily speculative.
47. This affiliation is given by the thirteenth-century Ghurid historian Jūzjānī and must have arisen when the Ghaznavids had become considerably Persianised in culture if not in ethnos; see Bosworth 1973: 61.

4

Economy and Society in Early Islamic Iran:
A Moment in World History

Richard W. Bulliet
(Professor of Middle Eastern History, Columbia University)

The rise and fall of a bourgeois Iranian society in the early Islamic centuries does not feature in anyone's narrative of world history. The closest approximation is in Richard N. Frye's book *The Golden Age of Persia*, subtitled *The Arabs in the East*.[1] But even there, the seeming contradiction between the title and the subtitle epitomises the problem of representing Iranian history between the fall of the Sasanian empire in 29 AH/650 CE and roughly the year 493 AH/1100 CE. Should the extraordinary flourishing of Iran's highland plateau be ascribed to the Arabs who invaded, or to the native Iranians? To Muslims exclusively, or to the society as a whole? Is the cultural dynamism to be read only in Arabic texts, or in Persian writings as well? Only in books by Muslims, or also in the writings of Zoroastrians, Christians, and Jews?

The practice of historians has long been to subordinate the story of Iran in this time period to the story of Islam. The militant movement that overthrew the unimpeachably Arab caliphal dynasty of the Umayyads in 308 AH/750 CE came from Iranian territory and engaged many Iranian converts to Islam in both its leadership and its soldiery. Yet it is represented primarily as a turning point in the history of Islam. The Abbasid dynasty that was the beneficiary of this movement gradually adopted many of the ceremonial, administrative, and cultural practices of the Iranian Sasanian regime that had succumbed to the Arab invaders a century earlier. Yet this is most often seen as symptomatic of Islam's capacity for absorbing and breathing new life into the traditions of its diverse peoples. The personalities, forces, and controversies that shaped the developing institutions of the Islamic religion did not just play out on the Baghdad stage, but also in burgeoning cities throughout Iran. Yet insofar as the language in which these controversies are recorded was almost exclusively Arabic, their historical moment is elided with that of the Arab Muslims whose extraordinary conquests had brought Iran into the caliphal empire.

All of these representations are valid when seen through the prism of Islamic history, of course, although they are somewhat less valid as part of

Arab history since specialists on matters Arabian frequently forget to mention how many of the most prominent authors of medieval works in Arabic grew up in Persian-speaking homes. In either case, however, what is missing is any narrative of the cotton boom that transformed the Iranian heartland and sparked an unprecedented surge of urbanisation between 132 AH/750 CE and 390 AH/1000 CE, or of the subsequent undoing of much of that transformation as a consequence of a sharp chilling of the climate between 390 AH/1000 CE and 696 AH/1200 CE. (The detailed evidence for this unsuspected succession of boom and bust is contained in my forthcoming book, *Cotton, Climate, and Camels in Early Islamic Iran: a moment in world history.*[2])

A politically oriented historian might cite the lack of a centralised Iranian state, and Iran's actual incorporation in an empire centred on Iraq, as adequate explanation for a perspective skewed toward Islam and the Arabs. After all, when the temporal power of the caliphate began to erode in the ninth century CE, several parts of Iran became wholly or partially independent under ruling houses of Iranian ethnic origin: Tahirids, Saffarids, Samanids, Ziyarids, Buyids. The importance of these successor states, and of such specifically Iranian characteristics as their use of pre-Islamic symbolism and patronage of Persian-language writings, has been amply and properly recognised.[3] But since no successor state succeeded in establishing itself over most of Iran until the Oghuz Turkomans created the Seljuq sultanate in the eleventh century CE, the separate histories of these ethnically Iranian principalities, which were frequently at war with one another, cannot easily be summed to a history of Iran as a whole.

By shifting the analytical focus to the economic and social sphere, the evolution of Iran as a whole becomes much more visible. The data to support this shift of focus are sparse, discontinuous, and subject to interpretive debate, but the picture they present fits well with the more conventional political narratives. Moreover, the drama of Iran's boom and bust is so startling that it raises new and unsuspected questions about Iran's impact of world history in general.

Comprehensive histories of Iran through the ages lavish attention on a series of pre-Islamic empires: Achaemenids, Seleucids, Parthians, Sasanians.[4] But in every one of these instances, the capital province of the empire was Mesopotamia, usually focused on a city in the Baghdad area, and the surviving political narratives provide the greatest detail in accounts of conflicts with foes coming from west of Mesopotamia: Greeks, Phoenicians, Romans, Byzantines. Information about the Iranian plateau is rare; without archaeology almost nothing would be known. This could simply be the result of poor preservation of history works dealing with the area, but it seems more likely that the aristocratic society of the plateau paid more attention to the legends and tales that were eventually brought together in the *Shāhnāma*, than to the annals of real kings.

The fragments of narrative and array of archaeological artifacts reflective of life in the plateau region are consistent with the image of a rural aristocracy living quite grandly, a village-based grain-growing economy with very little urbanisation, and a role in the imperial polity of supplying cavalry for the armies of the kings. Oddly enough, this description is not far from the image of Iran in the post-Seljuq period down to around 905 AH/1500 CE, except for a dramatic increase during those later centuries in pastoral nomadism; a persistence of city life, though on a reduced scale from its heyday in the tenth century CE; and the disappearance of Mesopotamia as the imperial centre to which the society of the plateau is subordinate. As the general histories make clear, the horse warriors of the Seljuq and post-Seljuq era generally fight for rulers who are based in Iran proper.

How does a historian assess, then, the centuries intervening between the fall of the Sasanians and the rise of the Seljuqs, when Iran became suddenly transformed into one of the world's most productive and dynamic urban societies? Before addressing this question, let us take a more general look at the transformation without delving into the complex methodological and data-processing questions that are needed to substantiate that look.

When the Arab invasions brought the Sasanian Empire to a surprisingly swift end, the invaders had no particular plan for what would come next. Different conquered regions adapted to the change of regime in different ways, partly depending on the decisions made by the Muslim leadership about where to station armies and where to focus their tax administration. In the Iranian plateau region, the economy that the Arabs gained control of was primarily agricultural with most people living in more-or-less self-sufficient farming villages. There was also a substantial transit trade, much of it in luxury goods, along the Silk Road, the route linking Mesopotamia, and the Mediterranean coast farther to the west, with Central Asia and China. This trade was anchored by a number of small, walled, garrison towns, though caravan cities like Bukhara and Samarkand farther to the east beyond the Oxus River were larger and commonly the foci of small independent principalities.

The fact that Arab armies campaigned as far east as Kyrgyzstan, more than 2000 miles from their desert homeland, while elsewhere stabilising their borders much closer to familiar territory, to wit, along the Taurus Mountain frontier of southern Anatolia and at the first cataract of the Nile in Egypt, indicates that the new rulers fully understood the importance of the Silk Road trade. In all likelihood, some Arab merchants or stockbreeders had even participated in the trade before the Muslims came along, or before they themselves became Muslims.

The conquests not only brought to power a new ruling elite, but they also delivered large quantities of money into Arab hands in the form of booty, military pay, and tax revenues. Unlike Iraq, Egypt, and Tunisia, where the Arab presence was concentrated in large military encampments, or Palestine and Syria, which were contiguous to traditional tribal grazing lands in the Arabian desert, Muslim rule in Iran operated through smaller army garrisons spotted at a number of strategic locales, particularly in the plateau region. Gorgan on the lowland plain at the southeast corner of the Caspian Sea received more Arabs than most other places because it guarded the Karakum Desert frontier that separated Iran from the lands of the Turks to the north, and Marv received the largest force because it protected the Oxus as well as the Karakum frontier. Farther to the east, a large Arab garrison at Balkh anchored Muslim control in northern Afghanistan and the mountainous lands north of the Oxus. All of this took place before the year 750 CE.

The survival of an early local history for the city and district of Qom, one of the smaller Arab settlements, allows us to address the question of how the newcomers adapted economically to life in Iran. There is every reason to believe that the economic and agricultural situation in Qom was paralleled in other piedmont districts, though the local political circumstances of its Arab community in Qom were atypical. Looking for a place to invest their money — my apologies for the anachronistic modern terminology — certain Arab entrepreneurs, almost certainly Yemenis by origin since that was the dominant Arab group, hit on the idea of digging *qanat*s, i.e., underground irrigation tunnels, and creating new villages devoted to the cultivation of cotton, a crop that had long been grown in Yemen but was new to the Iranian plateau.

Islamic law as it crystalised in the early Abbasid period, when these villages were coming to being, included a 'homestead' provision that granted freehold ownership to people who brought uncultivable land into production. Founding new villages in areas of desert watered by newly dug *qanat*s thus provided an avenue for intrusive Arabs to become landowners without contesting land rights with the much more numerous Iranian landowners. The policies adopted by the Muslim rulers allowed the latter to continue in possession of their own villages. Piedmont Iran's geography and long established techniques of *qanat* excavation opened up this new avenue of agricultural exploitation in a way that could not easily be imitated in other conquest areas. Farther west in the Zagros Mountains, or farther east in stretches of arable land along the Tejen, Murghab, Oxus, and Zeravshan rivers, Arab settlers seem to have found other sorts of opportunity. But the information particular to Qom is particularly revealing.

To repay the high cost of *qanat* and village construction, the new entrepreneurs, which included a minority of non-Muslims, planted summer crops instead of grain. Wheat and barley, the mainstay of Sasanian agriculture, were normally grown on rain-fed, spring-fed, or runoff-irrigated land that did not require so great an investment in irrigation. They were also traditionally winter crops, as is symbolised by the age-old Nauruz ('New Year' = vernal equinox) custom of ceremonially displaying sprouting wheat, which, as a summer crop, would not even have been planted by the third week in March. Pomegranates, apricots, melons, and vegetables for local consumption were appropriate for irrigated gardens close to towns; but the ideal crop for somewhat more distant villages was cotton.

In terms of total acreage, cotton did not come close to displacing grain. But as in Egypt, India, and the American South at other moments in history, cotton had the capability of transforming the country's manufacturing and trading economy. Cotton had to be freed of seeds, cleaned, combed, spun into thread, and woven into cloth. Dying, bleaching, fulling, and tailoring were also involved, depending on the fabric being produced. These industrial processes entailed a higher concentration of labour and a more specialised division of labour than farming villages could normally supply, and the transport and marketing of finished products similarly depended on well-developed distribution systems. Thus the emergence of cotton as an agricultural commodity provided an economic impetus for the governing points in which the Arabs had planted garrisons to expand into towns and cities. Unlike the cities that had protected the Silk Road caravans in the previous era, these new urban centres were based on the manufacturing and export of textiles.

In Sasanian times, cotton farming and cotton cloth had been virtually unknown in the plateau region, though it had already been introduced into some of the river-irrigated urban centres of Central Asia on a fairly minor scale through contacts with India. By the early ninth century CE, however, cotton was already developing into the economic mainstay of an Arab-Muslim society that no longer occupied itself primarily with military operations. The evidence of distinctive place-names in the Qom region at this time indicates that non-Muslim village owners continued to devote their efforts to growing winter wheat and barley.[5]

As investment in cotton farming became the preferred enterprise of the local Muslim elite, which gradually grew to include a larger and larger number of Iranian converts to Islam, cotton acquired a strong doctrinal association with Islam. Learned Muslims in Iran, a large proportion of whom, apparently around 40 percent, were engaged in or funded from one or another aspect of cotton production, popularized anti-silk and implicitly pro-cotton teachings, such as the following:

Ibn Abi Laila narrated:

> While Hudhaifa was at al-Mada'in [*i.e.*, in the Baghdad area], he asked for water whereupon the chief of the village brought him water in a silver cup. Hudhaifa threw it at him and said, I have thrown it only because I have forbidden him to use it, but he does not stop using it. The Messenger of God said, 'Gold, silver, silk and *dibaj* [silk brocade] are for them [the unbelievers] in this world and for you [Muslims] in the Hereafter.' [Bukhari, *Sahih*, 7:722]

Some of these prescriptive *hadith*s they traced directly to the prophet Muhammad and others to early Arab responses to encounters with the defeated Sasanian elite. Religious precepts thus encouraged a rapid growth in cotton consumption as new converts to Islam sought to emulate the flowing, plain-cloth style of dress of the Arabs and the earliest converts. Sasanian-era silk brocades, a major component of Silk Road trade, remained popular among the elite strata of the majority non-Muslim population. Silk also came into fashion among some members of the Muslim civil elite, particularly in Baghdad, who emulated the luxuries of their predecessors; but the religious prohibitions were officially honoured nevertheless through the caliphal government's establishment of *tiraz* factories. The plain cotton (and in Egypt linen) fabrics with a single line of calligraphic silk embroidery produced in these factories for fabrication into official robes of honour made explicit the connection between Islam and textile preferences.

A visible competition arose between a Muslim lifestyle and a non-Muslim lifestyle, particularly in the growing cities. This was manifested not just in clothing preferences, but also in ceramics. Muslim austerity and reverence for the Arabic script contrasted dramatically with Sasanian luxury and figurative ornamentation. Nishapur ware and Samarkand ware, essentially identical types of plain white dishes ornamented with bands of black or aubergine calligraphy achieved great popularity and became a pottery equivalent of *tiraz* that was affordable by Iran's newly forming bourgeoisie. Cotton probably also contributed directly to the spread of Islam. It is likely that the farmers attracted to work in the new cotton villages were classified as Muslims, and dressed like Muslims, regardless of their private convictions or depth of knowledge of the Muslim faith.

The differential between tax rates on grain and on cotton shows that growing cotton was highly profitable. The fact that Iraq was geographically unsuited to growing cotton because of the uncontrollable spring floods on the Tigris and Euphrates rivers enhanced this profitability since Arabs and new converts there bought cloth imported from Iran. The cotton boom fueled exuberant growth in the size of Iran's cities during the ninth and tenth centuries CE. It provided money for urban construction and land speculation; it provided employment in textile manufacturing; and it encouraged new converts to migrate to the cities and share in the Islam-focused prosperity. Never before had a domestically produced industrial commodity played such an important role in the overall Iranian economy, or competed in importance with the products carried by Silk Road caravans. Now, instead of the Silk Road products all going to Mesopotamia, Iran's own cities became marketing points.

The scholarly elite (*ulama*) of the Muslim community, through their religious endorsement of cotton consumption and deep involvement in its production, stood at the centre of urbanization and commerce. Through their own enterprise or through intermarriage, the most illustrious scholarly lineages had acquired, by the late tenth century CE, such significant commercial and landowning interests that they constituted a patrician class that dominated local urban society and politics, though more on the pattern of the patrician elites of late medieval Europe than of the earlier, legally defined, Roman patriciate. And their tastes and consumption patterns bespoke a bourgeois outlook that was far different both from that of the old Sasanian rural gentry and from the humble farmers who had toiled in the aristocrats' villages. To be sure, many *ulama* families had commercial interests other than, or in addition to, cotton; but the wearing of plain white cotton (or linen) became the hallmark of the religious profession, and continues to be so to the present day.

A biographical note about an eminent scholar from Gorgan epitomizes this development. After praising Abu Sa'd al-Isma'ili (d. 397 AH/1007 CE) for his erudition in Arabic and Islamic law, his piety, and his generosity, the biographer writes:

> Among those things by which God blessed him was that when his death drew near, all of what he possessed by way of wealth and estates departed him. He had sent cotton to Bab al-Abwab [Darband on the western side of the Caspian Sea]; it was all lost at sea. He had goods that were being transported from Isfahan; Kurds descended upon them and took them. He had some wheat being shipped to him from Khorasan; a group of people fell upon it and plundered it. He had an estate in the village known as Kuskara; Qabus b. Wushmagir [Gorgan's ruler at that time] ordered that its trees be uprooted, and they were. The *qanat* was filled in and all his property seized.[6]

Iran's creative urban culture continued to evolve even as the cotton boom waned in the tenth century CE. Centuries-old traditions do not easily pass away, and the landowning families that joined the Muslim community in great numbers in the late ninth and early tenth centuries CE saw no reason to ape the Arabs just because the prophet Muhammad happened to have been born in Mecca.[7] By this time the caliphate had lost political control, and local rulers of Iranian descent had taken power in most parts of Iran. With them, pre-Islamic styles and tastes reappeared, and the Persian language enjoyed a literary revival. In the cities, society became more complex. Some patrician families retained attitudes rooted in earlier, Arab-centreed, Muslim practice; others favored newer attitudes and practices that were more responsive to the indigenous Iranian population, and more welcoming to new converts. This division contributed to a growing current of factional conflict even though the nominal basis of the contestation was differing Sunni views on Islamic law.

Cotton continued to be a mainstay of the manufacturing and export economy, but among the civil elite it had certainly lost its cachet as a preferred clothing textile by the mid-tenth century CE. Silk brocade was back. At the same time, city growth through rural-urban migration, partly prompted by conversion and partly by economic opportunity, was reaching a point where the surplus food production of an increasingly labour-starved countryside was barely enough to sustain the populations of non-productive urbanites. In some regions, such as the area around Nishapur in Khorasan, the percentage of the population living in the ten largest cities became comparable to the rate found in northern Italy and Flanders, the most highly urbanised parts of Europe. Unlike their European counterparts, however, Iran's plateau cities did not have the benefit of inexpensive water transport for bringing foodstuffs from distant growing regions.[8] It is noteworthy that in the litany of troubles that beset Abu Sa'd al-Isma'ili at the end of his life was the loss of wheat imported from Khorasan. The price of wheat in Gorgan, normally a rich agricultural area, must have been quite high to offset the cost of transporting such a bulky product over more than a hundred miles of mountainous road.

Instances of drought and crop failure became increasingly perilous, apparently to the extent of leading governments to slash the tax rates on wheat and barley in an effort to get landowners with *qanat*-irrigated fields to abandon cotton for grain and thus help sustain the basic food production. To the extent that this dramatic lowering of taxes — from 15 silver coins per land unit to a tenth that number between 183 AH/ 800 CE and 286 AH/ 900 CE, with the rate on cotton staying even at 30 silver coins — may have successfully induced a partial shift from cotton to grain farming, it would have inevitably touched the economic life of the cities by reducing the volume of cotton manufactures and exports.

Though a string of bad winters in the second quarter of the tenth century CE gave northern Iran a taste of what a major change in the weather might bring, the Big Chill, a climatic shift of 130 years duration indicated by tree-ring records from western Mongolia,[9] did not set in until the eleventh century CE. By that time, the bourgeois life-style fostered in large part by the cotton boom, and manifested in the social dominance of the patrician class, was already showing signs of stress. Factional feuding along religious lines had become endemic, and leading patrician families were sometimes bitterly at odds with one another. Episodes of famine and disease seem to have become more numerous, but the historical narratives are too spotty to be sure that this was the case.

A sense of how intense this weather change was may be gained from the following sampling of reports in the historical sources:

> On November 24, 398 AH/ 1007 CE snow fell in Baghdad. It accumulated to one *dhira'* in one place and to one-and-a-half *dhira'* in another. [A *dhira'* is a unit of length equal to the average distance from elbows to fingertips.] It stayed on the ground for two weeks without melting. People shoveled it from their roofs into the streets and lanes. Then it began to melt, but traces of it remained in some places for almost twenty days. The snowfall extended to Tikrit [80 miles to the north], and letters arrived from Wasit [100 miles to the south] mentioning the fall there between Batiha and Basra, Kufa, Abadan, and Mahruban.[10]

> 1098/492 AH/ 1098 CE: In Khorasan, there was a sharp increase in prices, with food prices becoming impossible. It lasted for two years. The reason was cold weather that entirely destroyed the crops. Afterward the people were visited by pestilential disease. A large number of them died making it impossible to bury them all.[11]

> A letter written in the year 500 AH/1106 CE by the famous theologian al-Ghazzali to the Seljuq ruler, Sultan Sanjar: 'Be merciful to the people of Tus [al-Ghazzali's hometown near Nishapur in Khorasan], who have suffered boundless injustice, whose grain was destroyed by cold and drought, and whose hundred year old trees dried up at the

> roots . . . For if you demand something from them, they will all flee and die in the mountains.'[12]

No continuous record of weather or famine reports is available to verify with absolute certainty the indications of the Mongolian tree-ring evidence, but the eleventh century CE was unquestionably a period of profound change. Historical narratives reliably inform us of an unprecedented movement of the Oghuz Turkomans from Central Asia into Iran. Though the stereotype of Central Asian nomadic society focuses on horse herding, the tribes that entered Khorasan at this time herded both horses and one-humped camels. Being essential for military purposes, the former probably outnumbered the latter. But the camels provided an important economic link with the caravan trade along the Silk Road. The Oghuz pastoralists interbred their herds of one-humped females with a few two-humped males to produce unusually large and strong animals — *bukht* the male, *jammaza* the female — that were ideal for carrying loads or, in the case of females, for soldiers riding through desert terrain. The traditional lands of the Oghuz were located in the northern reaches of the Karakum Desert west of Khwarazm, the arable delta region where the Oxus River flowed into the Aral Sea. The new lands they sought in their migrations were on the considerably warmer southern fringe of the same desert.

Exactly why the Turkomans were allowed to enter Khorasan is unclear, but Sultan Mahmud of Ghazna, who authorised their relocation, probably assumed that they would fit reasonably well into the economy as producers of valuable livestock. On the Oghuz side, the cooling of the climate must have enhanced their desire to relocate, if it was not the sole rationale, since the available information on one-humped camels of that era indicates that they had difficulty surviving during cold winters. As it turned out, these first Turkoman immigrants turned to pillaging, and some of them were driven away by the Ghaznavid army. Continuing livestock problems may well have contributed to this since instead of returning to Central Asia, or moving back north to Khwarazm, many of them made their marauding way deeper into Iran. Ultimately they found their way into Anatolia.

The next wave of Oghuz also petitioned to move from the northern Karakum to the warmer south in exactly the same places the earlier wave had settled in, a string of desert fringe locales — Dehistan, Farava, Nisa, Sarakhs — currently in southern Turkmenistan. So it is likely that if the first wave had been experiencing livestock problems, the second wave would too. Fearing a repetition of the pillaging carried out by the earlier migrants, Sultan Mahmud's son Mas'ud forced the new group, led by the Seljuq family, into a military confrontation. Sultan Mas'ud lost the crucial battle of Dandanqan and ceded Khorasan to the Seljuqs.

Unlike the Oghuz who had preceded them, or the Oghuz who ravaged Khorasan more than a century later after inflicting a surprise defeat on Sultan Sanjar, the last powerful Seljuq ruler, in 1153/547, the tribes /men/ that the Seljuqs led into Khorasan remained disciplined and helped the new rulers build a unified and comparatively peaceful domain extending from Iraq to northern Afghanistan. As for the economy, the noted historian Ann Lambton has written:

> The Saljuq invasion does not appear to have caused a major break in the general continuity of rural prosperity.[13]

However, the supporting evidence cited in her accompanying discussion mostly concerns southern Iran, which was less affected by the Big Chill. Khorasan, she admits, declined significantly in importance. Seljuq land policies featured increased reliance on land grants (*iqta'*) in return for military or government service. This may have temporarily raised revenues by giving the grantees licence to oppress the peasantry — note the indication of overtaxing in al-Ghazzali's letter cited above — but it would have done nothing to restore flagging production in areas facing environmental deterioration. Nor is it likely to have encouraged landowners to invest more in their properties.

The superior leadership of the Seljuq family probably stemmed from prior involvement with caravan trading along the Silk Road. Like the Mongols of the thirteenth century, the Seljuqs focused their economic attention on long-distance trade. Among other effects, this served to popularize artistic styles and techniques derived from Chinese models and to encourage the growth of luxury consumption in ruling circles.

The undeniable prosperity of early Seljuq times could not conceal the fact that the agricultural infrastructure of northern Iran was suffering badly from nomadic incursions, rural insecurity, government neglect, and (especially) the Big Chill. Most cities suffered severe factional discord. The factional enmity dated from the tenth century, but its increasingly violent manifestations bespeak a competition for material resources that were becoming increasingly scarce and unreliable.

By the early twelfth century, northern Iran was in a declining condition. Members of patrician families that had the necessary financial means and scholarly connections outside Iran migrated to Iraq, Syria, Anatolia, or India. The patrician-dominated bourgeois market that had shaped consumption in pre-Seljuq times faded away, and Iran entered a long period of minimal contribution to the religious culture of Islam. The inability of the Khwarazmshahs to restore prosperity and order after Sanjar's reign highlights the degree of damage Iran suffered during the Big Chill. By then warmth had returned, but Iran's human and economic resources were too depleted to permit any significant recovery before the Mongol onslaught.

On a world scale, Iran's moment of flowering had five significant impacts that have no parallel in earlier or later Iranian history. First, Mesopotamia under the Abbasid caliphs became the centre of a vast economic region stretching from Central Asia to Tunisia instead of being the eastern border of the lands around the Mediterranean. The wealth in silver dirhams derived from taxation and commerce in the lands to the east of the Zagros mountains exceeded the wealth in gold *dinar*s derived from the older urbanised economies of Syria,

Palestine, Egypt, and North Africa. Where the various pre-Islamic dynasties that ruled from Mesopotamia between 500 BCE and the beginning of the Arab conquests had repeatedly sought to expand westward, the Muslim state paid much greater attention to eastern affairs. No Abbasid caliph ever set foot in Egypt, Palestine, or coastal Syria; and Tunisia was the first province to be granted autonomy — in return for an annual tribute payment — by the Baghdad caliphs shortly after the year 183 AH/800 CE. By contrast, the first ten Abbasid rulers were all deeply involved in military campaigns or political machinations on the Iranian plateau, and several of them, e.g., al-Mahdi, Harun al-Rashid, al-Ma'mun, and al-Mu'tasim, spent substantial amounts of time there.

One reflection of this eastern orientation was a change in the locus of trading momentum. The Silk Road had always found its primary western terminus in one of a series of Mesopotamian capitals from Babylon to Ctesiphon that were built near the point where the Tigris and Euphrates rivers flow nearest to one another. Baghdad proved to be the last of these. But under earlier dynasties, substantial quantities of Silk Road goods had moved on up the Euphrates by caravan to find their way into Mediterranean commerce, usually being sold at entrepôts like Dura Europus or Palmyra located near the frontier between a state based in Mesopotamia and some rival to the west. The early Islamic centuries, however, saw no great trading centres in those areas, nor does it appear that merchants in Syria, Egypt, or Byzantine Anatolia traded very extensively with Baghdad. It seems, rather, that the growing prosperity of urban Iran created an expanded outlet for Silk Road commodities that in earlier centuries had simply transited across northern Iran by caravan without being subject to much market activity at intermediate points. The upshot of this development is that the preferences and styles of the people living in the cities on the Iranian plateau region became defining components of the emergent Abbasid culture of Islam.

Secondly, Egypt, Palestine, and Syria were so overshadowed by Iran that they hold a comparatively negligible place in the history of the Middle East between 132 AH/750 CE and 493 AH/1100 CE. This had never happened before since the advent of the pharaohs, and it was not to happen again after the undermining of the Iranian economy by the Big Chill allowed the coastlands of the Mediterranean to resume the paramount role in the Middle East that they continue to play to the present day. It is symptomatic of this diminished status that the only truly important Muslim political phenomenon at the eastern end of the Mediterranean after 132 AH /750 CE, the rise and fall of the Fatimid state in Tunisia, Egypt, and coastal Syria between 296 AH /909 CE and 566 AH /1171 CE, defined itself in opposition to Abbasid Baghdad, both politically and doctrinally, but never acquired the power to mount a credible military challenge.

How different medieval Mediterranean history might have been if Baghdad's rulers, and their local successors in various parts of Iran, had cared about what happened in the west. Spain went its separate way. Tunisia's conquest of Sicily did not interest people in the east. The Fatimid takeover of

Tunisia, Algeria, and Morocco was a far off event of little note until the new Isma'ili Shi'ite counter-caliphate successfully expanded into Egypt and parts of Syria. And even then, the Isma'ilis in Iran — the Assassins — loomed as a more potent threat in the imaginations of men of affairs in Mesopotamia and Iran.

Would greater attention to the affairs of Muslims living to the west of the Syrian-Iraqi desert have meant a stronger, more coordinated, and more aggressive attitude toward Christian Europe? Would it have enlivened Mediterranean trade? Would it have enhanced Europe's awareness of and concerns about Islam? There is no way of telling. But it is strikingly apparent that the eleventh century, when climate change triggered widespread economic difficulty in Iran accompanied by nomadisation, urban decline, and the emigration of the learned elite, also saw a marked revival of economic, cultural, and political interaction among the various Muslim and Christian principalities bordering on the Mediterranean. It is not inconceivable that the Mediterranean revival depended in some measure on the waning of Iran's dynamism.

The third broad impact of Iran's moment in the sun was that it forever changed the template of life on the plateau. Though nomads would from time to time ravage the land and bring down ruling dynasts, the idea of Iran as a land of cities never disappeared. Even when landowners enjoying royal favour came to control scores of villages, the pre-Islamic pattern of a warrior aristocracy settled in a dispersed fashion throughout the countryside never returned. The new landowners were either tribal chieftains, in which case they might indeed live in the country, but as pastoralists, or else they chose to live in or near town and send their agents to collect rents from their villages. To this day, Iranians identify themselves by the urban centre of the region they come from and by its traditional customs and local manufactures. They prefer city names like Shirazi or Tabrizi to regional epithets like Farsi or Azerbaijani. Without the urbanisation of the ninth/third and tenth/fourth centuries, this pattern would not have been there to guide the country's recovery in the fifteenth century after a century of Mongol rule and the renewed disruptions of the Timurid era.

Language is the fourth area of impact. Every historian of Iran and of Islam has speculated on the reason or reasons for the failure of Arabic to achieve the dominance in Iran that it gained in the other regions conquered in the initial Islamic conquests. New Persian, a streamlined *koiné* written in Arabic script, first appeared during the period of Iran's economic boom; and great works of literature were already being authored in this language by the time the Big Chill set in the eleventh century. This did not mean, however, that the several Middle Iranian languages of pre-conquest times — Middle Persian, Parthian, Sogdian, Bactrian, Khwarezmian, etc... — promptly disappeared. Indeed, Yaghnobi, a modern descendant of Sogdian, is still spoken in parts of Tajikistan. So not only was New Persian distinctive in its use of the Arabic script, but it saturated and lent linguistic uniformity to an Iranian language zone that had previously been multi-lingual and politically divided among a number of principalities.

Religion, as symbolised by the Arabic script, is the ostensible common denominator underlying this newfound linguistic uniformity. Zoroastrians continued to write religious books in Middle Persian using a pre-conquest script. But to the degree that Islam had anything to say doctrinally about language, it favoured Arabic, the language of the Qur'an. Moreover, the religious elite of the Muslim community preferred for many generations to write in Arabic, leaving New Persian, at least initially, to poets, storytellers, and historians. References to Islam or its teachings are uncommon in the corpus of earliest compositions in New Persian. However, that corpus is quite small and consists mostly of poems and romances prior to the tenth century.

An alternative common denominator could be the urban-based economic linkages that grew out of the cotton boom that began at the beginning of the ninth century. Muslims played the dominant role in building the new economy and populating the growing cities. They also became the most active participants in overland trade as they transported cotton cloth (and other goods) from as far east as Samarkand toward the great consumption centre of Baghdad. New Persian, therefore, may have arisen the way Swahili and Bahasa Indonesia did in later periods of Islamic history, namely, as the language of merchants who resorted to a simplified grammar and morphology to gloss over the differences among the Middle Iranian tongues used in various localities, and who found an easy way to incorporate Arabic loan words by adopting the Arabic script. Known to all literate Muslims, but probably not to most non-Muslim Iranians, the Arabic script would similarly have afforded a means of overriding the preceding diversity of Middle Iranian writing systems.

Looking at the innovators of New Persian as a newly rising class of Muslim merchants and manufacturers responding to a pressing need to communicate with their counterparts in other parts of the Iranian cultural zone would help explain the uniformity, simplicity, and broad geographical extent of the new tongue. And it would also raise the possibility that the Arabic script was deliberately intended to define a specifically Muslim commercial and cultural network. However, linking the emergence of New Persian to the cotton boom is entirely speculative. No commercial writings have survived from the period in any language, and the number of Iranian poets known to have written in Arabic dwarfs the handful who experimented with Persian.

By contrast, linking the decline of the Iranian agricultural economy in the era of the Big Chill to the spread outside Iran of New Persian is fairly obvious. No New Persian authors are known to have worked outside Iran prior to the Seljuq period, but by the thirteenth century both Anatolia and India were known for the exquisite Persian verses composed there by Jalal al-Din Rumi (d. 1273/671 AH/1273 CE) and Amir Khusrau (d. 725 AH/1325 CE) respectively. What is important about these master poets for present purposes is not their life histories or the content of their verses but the fact that they rhapsodized for Persian-speaking audiences and had Persian-speaking colleagues and imitators in these foreign lands. So far as is known, the pre-Islamic Iranian dynasties never exported their languages to other lands. Not even to Mesopotamia, which was under Iranian rule for most of the millennium preceding the Arab conquests. What supported the spread of New Persian from the Seljuq era onward was not just the military success of the Turkoman warriors in Anatolia and Afghan tribesmen in northern India, but also the migration out of Iran of scholars and *litterateurs* relocating themselves in response to deteriorating conditions in their homeland. To be sure, the Mongol invasion in the early thirteenth century put a capstone on Iran's decline and forced many people to flee the destruction of their cities and not just the freezing of their crops. But there is ample evidence that the Iranian diaspora was well underway before the Mongols arrived. And there is similarly ample evidence that the emergence of New Persian as a cosmopolitan language of administration and culture from the Bay of Bengal to the Aegean Sea left a telling mark on world history.

The fifth and final impact of Iran's boom and bust lies in the area of religion. In the sixteenth century, under the aegis of the Safavid dynasty, Iran became both declaratively and practically a Shi'ite land. Scholars disagree about how well implanted in the country Shi'ism was before the advent of the Safavids and on the extent of the coerced conversions that took place once the new identity was declared. All agree, however, that the interposition of a Shi'ite Iran between a Sunni Ottoman realm to the west, a Sunni Uzbek realm to the northeast, and a predominantly Sunni Muslim presence in India to the southeast powerfully shaped the history of the Muslim world from that time until the present.

From the ninth through the eleventh century, on the other hand, Iran was a predominantly Sunni land. To be sure, there are many indications that Shi'ites constituted a strong presence from time to time. The Buyid dynasty, for example, adhered first to the Zaidi and then to the Imami form of Shi'ism. And the Isma'ili movement attracted many believers, particularly in the time of the Big Chill. Nevertheless, any tally of writers, thinkers, and religious leaders for the period of rapid urbanisation and the cotton boom will come up with vastly more Sunnis than Shi'ites. Shi'ite *'ulama* maintained their own lists of leading scholars, but the tens of thousands of entries in the city-based biographical dictionaries that form a distinctive literary genre during this period — but not in later eras — are almost entirely Sunni and in aggregate are much more extensive than any Shi'ite compilation. Moreover, as the following table shows, the Sunni intellectual output of Iran overshadowed almost every other region of the caliphate during the boom period.

Ibn al-'Imad, whose biographical compilation of thousands of religious scholars provided the data for the table, was himself a Syrian living in the seventeenth century. His work, which covers the entire Muslim world for its first thousand years, is organised by death date, but for present purposes the dates have been thrown back sixty years to approximate birthdates. In his portrayal of the world of (Sunni) Muslim scholarship, the share of eminent religious personalities apportionable to Egypt and Syria combined never exceeds 20 percent prior to the late Seljuq period, but Iran alone has an average contribution of 40 percent for every quarter century period from 855/241

AH/855 CE to 491 AH/1097 CE. [14]

Dates	Total	IRAN	IRAQ	EG	SYR	EG+SY	Other
709/91	161	9%	46%	6%	12%	13%	27%
734/116	180	8%	61%	4%	13%	17%	14%
758/141	199	12%	62%	6%	12%	18%	8%
782/166	213	24%	54%	4%	10%	14%	8%
806/191	133	38%	39%	6%	13%	19%	4%
831/216	136	32%	48%	7%	4%	11%	9%
855/241	186	38%	39%	4%	10%	14%	8%
879/266	185	37%	39%	5%	12%	17%	7%
903/291	184	40%	36%	3%	10%	13%	11%
928/316	173	36%	42%	6%	8%	14%	8%
952/341	168	41%	32%	5%	10%	15%	12%
976/366	144	39%	31%	7%	12%	19%	11%
1000/391	123	51%	22%	4%	10%	14%	13%
1025/416	154	49%	29%	3%	6%	9%	13%
1049/441	127	39%	34%	4%	8%	12%	15%
1073/466	159	36%	33%	4%	11%	15%	16%
1097/491	151	32%	32%	5%	15%	20%	16%
1122/516	189	23%	37%	6%	20%	26%	14%
1146/541	193	23%	39%	7%	19%	26%	11%
1170/566	228	14%	29%	9%	38%	47%	10%
1194/591	192	6%	17%	11%	49%	60%	17%
1219/616	219	8%	12%	10%	60%	70%	10%

Table 1 - Regional representation among Muslim religious scholars.

The elite emigration that took place from the late eleventh century onward effectively stripped the Sunni mass of the population of its religious leadership while at the same time the factional discord and shrinking subsistence base of the cities in the north destroyed many of the mosques and seminaries (*madrasas*) that had nurtured that leadership. The *madrasa* as a dedicated centre for higher religious education had originated in Iran in the tenth century, if not before; and the institution had spread throughout the country before migrating into non-Iranian lands, more often than not with Iranian professors as inaugural academic directors. But by the beginning of the thirteenth century, there were few noteworthy seminaries still functioning, particularly in comparison with the many that were then flourishing in Iraq, Syria, Egypt, and elsewhere.

It could be argued, of course, that the famously destructive onslaught of the Mongols would have wiped out Iran's Sunni religious leadership even if it had not become depleted before Genghiz Khan's first invasion in 614 AH/1218 CE. But this would make it difficult to account for the continuing strong persistence of Sunni Islam in Central Asia, where the Mongol domination lasted even longer. It seems, rather, that the economically induced erosion of the Sunni spiritual leadership left Iran open to the much more populist and less legalistic guidance of Sufis, honored members of the family of Ali, and Shi'ite preachers who ascribed divinely ordained leadership to that family. In other words, the rise of Iranian Shi'ism was facilitated, though not caused, by the collapse of what had once been a powerful, wealthy, and highly institutionalised Sunni religious establishment.

The study of world history over the past thirty years has looked with favour upon Fernand Braudel's threefold division of time and causation: 'Events' are the happenings of any given moment and should not normally command the close attention of scholars interested in the grand scope of history. 'Conjunctures' occur when various forces and institutions come together in an often complex fashion to shape a new historical tendency over a period of decades or more. And the '*longue durée*' involves trends that are so drawn out chronologically as to be largely unnoticed at the time even though they can have a profound impact that lasts for centuries. Narratives concentrating on the last two of these historical dimensions commonly strive to look beyond traditional political boundaries and dynastic eras, but are sometimes criticised for depriving history of a human dimension.

The idea of a 'moment' in world history elides these three approaches. It concentrates on a particular place, the Iranian plateau, at a particular time, the ninth through twelfth centuries CE. Some of its arguments deal with humdrum events: the decisions made by agricultural entrepreneurs to invest in irrigation and grow cotton; or the decisions made by camel breeders to move their livestock to warmer pastures even in the face of military opposition. Other arguments are more conjunctural: the intersecting of religious teachings, economic benefit, and symbolic assertion of Muslim supremacy in the development of an urban-based cotton industry; or the coming together of agricultural decline, nomadisation of the countryside, and urban factional discord to prompt a far-reaching diaspora of Iran's religious and intellectual elite. Still others relate to the '*longue durée,*' notably the hypothesis that the northern Middle East experienced a Big Chill that lasted for more than a century.

From a world historical perspective, the impact of this moment was both complex and long lasting. But the story told here has been primarily the story of Iran in an era that is commonly given short shrift by historians. The economic and cultural efflorescence fostered by cotton production and rapid urbanization on the Iranian plateau in the first three Islamic centuries differed profoundly from anything that had happened in Iran before. And even though a change in climate brought an end to Iran's agricultural prosperity and exuberant bourgeois society, the traces of what the Iranians had created spread far and wide, and the land itself was left with a memory and a template of urban life that served as a base for revival in later and more propitious times. All in all, it was a moment to remember.

Notes:

1. Frye, 1975.
2. To appear in 2009 from Columbia University Press.
3. The most complete coverage, dynasty by dynasty, is in Frye, 1975a.
4. For recent one-volume examples see Daniel, 2000; Garthwaite, 2005; and Axworthy, 2008.
5. The highly technical analysis on which this statement is based is presented in full in Bulliet, 2009.
6. al-Sahmi, 1950: 134-135.
7. For a complete discussion of the rate of conversion to Islam and of its social impact see Bulliet, 1979. According to the analysis presented there, the most rapid growth period of Islam in Iran was the ninth century CE.
8. Bulliet, 1994: 136-137.
9. For data and analysis see my forthcoming book, *A Moment in World History*.
10. al-Jawzi, 1938-40: 237.
11. al-Athir, 1966: 291.
12. Krawulsky, 1975: 65. ed. I am most grateful to Dr. Kenneth Garden for this reference.
13. Lambton, 1973: 116.
14. The table was compiled from al-'Imad,1931-32.

5

Oranges, Quiddities and Algorisms

Lutz Richter-Bernburg
(Eberhard-Karls University, Tübingen)

In the far-flung territories of the caliphate or empire of Islam, an initial phase of military-political expansion, and closely following a second stage of consolidation of power and Arabisation of the subject peoples, provided the economic and socio-cultural background for an extraordinary outburst of severally productive activities among every single segment of the heterogeneous population. Their creative energies encompassed the most diverse fields of enterprise and study, whether it was religious devotion and reflection, military power and glory, learning and scholarship, or more mundane pursuits like trade and commerce or arts and crafts. During the first three Islamic centuries the common medium of communication was the Arabic language. Whoever wanted to be abreast of things and participate in current debates had to master this idiom. At the same time — lest it be forgotten — some non-Muslim communities were spurred to increased literary production in their inherited languages as well. All in all, it cannot come as a surprise that the lands of Iran, a long-established centre of gravity in the political and cultural history of the pre-Islamic Near East, produced its share of torch-bearers of 'arts and sciences', not to speak of economic and commercial ventures by land and sea.

As is well-known, the political unity of the Islamic empire was not to last; progressive fragmentation led to the rise of regional, frequently short-lived dynasties and power centres where patronage of learning could also serve to shore up uncertain legitimacy and generally to strengthen rulership. In addition, through the first four centuries and in many cases much longer, regional particularism did not preclude the free flow of material and intellectual goods and merchandise across the vast expanse of the Islamic oecumene, from Transoxiana to the Pyrenees and from the Caucasus to sub-Saharan Africa — and beyond.

Even if commercial activities properly speaking are not included in the subject here under discussion, their Iranian dimension may briefly be highlighted with reference to a Hispano-Arabic traveller through western and central Europe around the year 961 CE. In the bustling market of the German town of Mainz, he was surprised to notice Samanid silver coins, minted in the years 913–914 CE, and oriental spices such as ginger, galingale and spikenard. Regardless of the precise itinerary of these Samanid drachms — plausibly through northeastern Europe — and of the non-Iranian origin of the three medicinal plants, the second of them, galingale, does reflect the Iranian stage of its far-travelled name between China and medieval Europe. Its earliest English attestation dates from around the year 1000,[1] i.e. less than half a century later than our Hispanic witness, Abraham Jacobson of Tortosa, if I may thus turn his Arabic name into modern English.[2]

The anecdotal evidence presented by Abraham of Tortosa and here gratefully acknowledged does not, however, as such indicate superior scientific activity in Iran in the period under discussion. Yet it may serve as an introduction to the vast corpus of writing in medicine and allied disciplines owed to authors of broadly defined Iranian background, and thus provide access to the first of three areas of scholarship I would like to concentrate on at present, the other two being philosophy and the mathematical disciplines. Obviously, from the point of view of ancient and medieval Aristotelianism, philosophy as such included mathematics and logic, in addition to 'physics' (i.e. all fields of inquiry into the sensible world), and finally metaphysics, inquiry into the intelligible world, into existence *qua* existence and epistemology. Medical learning, on the other hand, even though grounded in — Aristotelian — 'physics', was often disqualified from consideration as a full-fledged science, requiring as it did, practical application in either preserving or restoring health to individual, forever contingent, unknowable organisms.

To return for a moment to the three aromatic roots, ginger, galingale and spikenard, which our Tortosan traveller had encountered in Mainz, Asian vegetable substances, from fresh produce to dried and otherwise preserved spices and drugs, had been coveted and wherever possible, appropriated for cultivation, across Western Asia, the Mediterranean and Europe since antiquity. This process quickened in the period we are concerned with here, and at several levels. Clearly of most consequence was the actual introduction of new species into agri- and horticulture.[3] If it be permitted to dwell somewhat longer on the mentioned three aromatic roots, in my view, they do imply changes of much greater import. Already in the classical world, pharmacobotany and pharmacy, not to speak of agriculture as such and the culinary arts, had notably relied on much sought-after samples of Asian origin. With the translation and appropriation of classical science into the Islamic civilisation, and to a degree even earlier into pre-Islamic Iran, the legacy of ancient *materia medica* was acquired as well. However, Islamic dominions extending from the Indus to the Straits of Gibraltar, their population, and prominently among them medical practitioners and scholars were in a unique position to enrich the inherited knowledge and trading stock with hitherto unknown or ignored products — nor were they slow in doing so. This is where oranges fit in, and lemons, of course, as well as numerous other, unrelated plants and crops, not least among them staples like rice. Products and their names made their way across the Arabic world into Europe, either Sicily or the Iberian Peninsula, and from there northward. As for Persian *nāranj*, it lost its initial /n/ along its Arabic trajectory,[4] before taking on, as it were, a golden hue in French ('or') and entering into a mutual phonetic assimilation with the name of the Provençal city of Orange.

Evidently, not only edible merchandise was traded across continents, but intellectual property as well. The wealth of medical learning as produced in the lands of Islam and pre-eminently in Iran, did not have to overcome any internal borders, most of it being written in Arabic, the equivalent of Latin in medieval Roman Catholic Christianity.[5] During the first five centuries of Islam, until the eve of the crusades, the field of medicine and allied sciences was dominated by, but by no means the exclusive property of, authors from Iran,[6] if we except the translators from Greek into Arabic, and some notable writers from Egypt and the Maghrib. Also it should be remembered that Mesopotamia, with its mixed Aramaic — and Persian-speaking population, had been the central province of the Sasanian empire and under the Abbasid caliphate reasserted its rank. Three names stand out from among a host of other, not necessarily lesser, scholars:[7] in chronological sequence they are Abū Bakr ar-Rāzī (d. 925 CE/AH 313), ʿAlī b. al-ʿAbbās al-Majūsī (fl. 973–976 CE/AH 363–366, d. 994[?] CE/AH 384), and Abū ʿAlī ibn Sīnā (b. before 980 CE/AH 370, d. 1037 CE/AH 428). By no means is it owed to rhetorical conventions or the psychological impulse of inflating the importance of one's own subject or to an appeal to the audience's benevolence or a combination of the two motives if I add that this triad represents medieval learning and thought at the highest level, not only within the confines of Islamic civilisation. Actually, each one of them became known in Latin Europe by a latinised name, Rhazes, Haly Abbas and Avicenna, respectively. But I hasten to add that I do not mean to measure their rank by their subsequent reception, let alone by the fact that their works were translated into Latin or Hebrew, nor do I intend to apply the criteria of modern science to them. It is entirely against the foil of their own socio-cultural environment that their achievements are to be gauged, and it is by this yardstick that they are found exceptional. Again, this assertion is no expression of 'hero worship' since they were nourished and supported by the culture of a solid urban bourgeoisie. In the centuries here in focus, and especially between 850 and 1050, urban society in Iran produced an astounding number of artisans, poets and scholars of note. The rise of the neo-Persian language since the latter ninth century CE cannot be adequately assessed with reference to poetry alone, however brilliant its productions; prose, both narrative and scientific, equally has to be taken into account. Medicine, never merely an 'academic' pursuit, was a subject of Persian prose from the very beginning — as well as of didactic verse. The second half of the tenth century CE witnessed the appearance of textbooks for the medical practitioner in prose and epic verse and also the earliest *materia medica* in Persian;[8] it was no coincidence that these works originated in what was then eastern Iran, or differently put, the Samanid sphere of influence.[9] Yet even there, not to mention more westerly regions, the position of Arabic as the privileged idiom of scholarship remained unshaken. Neither ar-Rāzī nor al-Majūsī ever used Persian, and Avicenna did so only for a few more popular works.[10] Following Avicenna, it took the better part of another century, and the after-effects of the Seljuq Turkish invasion, for Persian to become the medium of medical learning on a par with Avicenna's classical work, the *Canon*.[11]

Concerning the position of Persian as a language of expository prose in the pre-Mongol period, I would like to submit the following observations. As noted above, Arabic remained the primary medium of expression although a 'Persianist' tendency advocating the elaboration of Persian for scholarly purposes can be detected in the first half of the eleventh century.[12] The great scholar al-Bīrūnī, to be discussed in more detail further on, spoke out rather acerbically against such attempts.[13] On the other hand, the use of Persian was given added impulse in the interest of Muslim, both mainstream and Isma'ili, missionary activities among the Turkic tribes of Central Asia and other groups not conversant with Arabic. Al-Bīrūnī's strictures against Persian can also serve to highlight the fact that the intellectual burgeoning of Iran in the period which Vladimir Minorsky once graphically if debatably called the 'Iranian *intermezzo*'[14] — between, respectively, Arab and Turkish domination — was most definitely bilingual, even predominantly Arabophone; Iranian identity was not in the least bound up with linguistic nationalism in a modern or contemporary sense.

But back to ar-Rāzī. As his name indicates, his family background was identified with the city of Ray, ancient Rhages/Rhaga, the functional predecessor of modern Teheran, whose southern suburbs have since engulfed the site of Ray's ruins. It was here as well as in the caliphal capital Baghdad that ar-Rāzī directed a hospital and engaged in a prodigious programme of writing.[15] While his fame mainly rests on his medical works, his philosophical ideas proving unpalatable to contemporaries and posterity alike, he deserves attention precisely for the audacity of his metaphysics and his — howsoever inchoate — notion of potentially open-ended scientific progress.[16] Clearly, the ideal of the physician-philosopher which ar-Rāzī strove to emulate had been inherited from Galen (d. 219 CE), the supreme medical role-model in Islam. In a different realization, we will encounter it again in Avicenna. In medicine, ar-Rāzī undertook to pass his knowledge to the most diverse audiences, from the consummate scholar to the lay person in need of a first-aid manual. His enormous collection of excerpts from a wide variety of earlier and contemporary authors is a monument to his encyclopaedic learning; it was posthumously gathered into a single multi-volume work. The history of its reception in Europe also deserves mention. In 1279, Sālim ibn Faraj, a Jewish physician from Agrigento, Sicily, presented his Latin translation, under the title of *Continens*, to Charles I of Anjou, king of Naples. As early as 1486, this Latin version was printed in a single huge folio volume in the northern Italian city of Brescia. At the other extreme of bulk, ar-Rāzī's monograph on *Smallpox and measles*, either one a continual scourge before the age of vaccination and modern hygiene, was repeatedly printed in Europe; as late as 1848, an English translation was published in London.[17]

The other two outstanding medical writers mentioned above, ʿAlī ibn al-ʿAbbās al-Majūsī[18] and Abū ʿAlī ibn Sīnā,[19] each authored a major work which was to gain long-lasting fame across boundaries of language, culture and religion, namely *al-Kitāb al-Malakī-kāmil aṣ-ṣināʿa aṭ-ṭibbīya* and *al-Qānūn fī t-ṭibb*. The former, having come to the attention of Constantine the African (d. 1085), was among the very first books of 'Arabic' (or 'Islamic', as in Marshall Hodgson's 'Islamicate') medicine to be adapted into Latin;[20] within half a century. Constantine's somewhat free version, inscribed *Pantegni*, drew such criticism that in 1127 Stephen of Pisa-Antioch retranslated it more faithfully, beginning with the title, *Regalis dispositio*.[21] Avicenna's medical *chef-d'œuvre*, *al-Qānūn fī t-ṭibb*,[22] travelled even further westward; in Toledo, Gerard of Cremona (d. 1187) prepared a Latin translation under the heading *Canon medicinae* which during the centuries to come, was to enjoy unsurpassed medical authority, in Latin Europe as well as in the Muslim world.[23]

Both ar-Rāzī and Ibn Sīnā were exemplary of the type of polymath so prominently represented in medieval civilisations; their activity as writers included numerous other fields in addition to medicine and philosophy, even though these contributed most to their respective fame. If the impact of Ibn Sīnā-Avicenna's *Canon* on European medicine still made itself felt long past the Renaissance, his philosophy too, for several centuries, was a major inspiration of Latin thought, particularly scholasticism. As is well known, during the twelfth century CE the Iberian Peninsula became the primary locale, of the Arabic-Latin interface, not least because of the Jewish presence in both the Arabic and the Romance linguistic domains.[24] Among the first philosophical texts to be 'Latinised' was Avicenna's treatise *De anima* ('On the soul') from his great Aristotelian encyclopaedia, *Liber Sufficientiae*, which elegantly if lopsidedly rendered *Kitāb ash-Shifāʾ* ('Book of the Cure/ Satisfaction').[25] Evidently, Avicenna's influence cannot be reduced to terms such as *quiddity*;[26] yet it clearly marks the degree to which Latin philosophical calques from Arabic were and have remained integrated into common English, in the process acquiring entirely novel meanings.[27] The Arabic exemplar, *māhīya* ('whatness', 'essence'), was not coined by Avicenna, but by a Graeco-Arabic translator of Aristotle and Plotinus a century and a half earlier, but in Avicenna's doctrine the concept of 'essence', as opposed to 'existence', gained vital importance; thus 'quiddity' in the Latin versions of his writings attained prominence too.[28]

As remarked above, the fact that an author remained unknown to the Latin Middle Ages can in no way be construed as prejudicial to his disciplinal rank; however towering a figure Avicenna may have been, he did not originate in a void and was surrounded and succeeded by serious co-contestants. From among his contemporaries, it may here suffice to name his aforementioned epistolary opponent Abū r-Rayḥān Muḥammad b. Aḥmad al-Bīrūnī (973 CE–past 1050 CE).[29] It was to the detriment of the Arabic west (*al-maghrib*) and Europe that his works remained unknown there, especially in view of the medieval Latins' interest in mathematics and astronomy; his great recast of Ptolemy's *Almagest*, *al-Qānūn al-Mas'ūdī* ('Canon for Masʿūd') and his treatise in mathematical geography, *Taḥdīd nihāyāt al-amākin li-taṣḥīḥ masāfāt al-masākin* ('Determination of the limits of places for the rectification of distances between settlements'), to name but two of his relevant titles, would have been worth all the attention his Maghribī and Latin audiences could have mustered. However, al-Bīrūnī cannot be viewed reductively as a mere mathematical specialist, however competent or even creative he may have been as such; transcending his positive achievements in a variety of fields, including — in his pioneering work on Hindu India — cultural anthropology and comparative religion, his claim to fame as one of the great scientists of all time rests on his overall critical attitude to received verities and on his — preliminary and tentative as it was — introduction of controlled experiments into scientific inquiry.

With al-Bīrūnī, we have approached the mathematical disciplines, the third domain of excellence in Iranian scholarship here to be discussed. From among the areas of 'science' cultivated in the first four to five centuries of Islam, and which radiated beyond the confines of Muslim polities, mathematics — obviously including starcraft — may have stood out for the impact which traditions from pre-Islamic Iran had on it — even if in turn, Iranian mathematics and allied fields on the eve of Islam were composed of elements of disparate regional-cultural origin — Greek, Mesopotamian, Indian and Iranian.[30] Furthermore, these components had, for varying lengths of time, been in more or less intensive interaction and exchange. Plausibly, it was their practical applications, whether in surveying, timekeeping or forecasting the future, which won them early entrance into the evolving Islamic civilisation. At any rate, when the caliph al-Manṣūr decided on a new capital, the foundation stone was laid in 762 CE/AH 145 on a day that a group of astrologers had elected as propitious.[31] It cannot come as a surprise that their leading figure, Nawbakht, was Iranian by education (and extraction), documenting both, as it were, by his very name, 'Newluck'.[32] Nor were his collaborators in catarchic astrology — in the given case, the election of a fortunate day (by 'hemerology') for the foundation of al-Manṣūr's 'City of Peace (Everlasting)' — aliens to the doctrines and operations of Sasanian starcraft; in fact, Sasanian traditions remained noticeable in the subsequent development of astrological literature in Arabic. Moreover the fact that technically sound astrology presupposed a solid command of mathematics was reflected in the multidisciplinary activity of many an astrological professional.[33] Thus the very al-Bīrūnī earned his livelihood as court astrologer, and it was in order to facilitate dissemination of his astrological textbook *at-Tafhīm* ('Effecting comprehension') that he may have deigned to use Persian. One name from among the many Iranian representatives of astrology may here be singled out, again on the basis of the rather extraneous circumstance of the Latin reception of his works, Abū Maʿshar Jaʿfar ibn Muḥammad al-Balkhī (172–273/787–886); his works on historical astrology and other astrological subjects made 'Albumasar' a household word in medieval Latin.[34]

During the first century of the Abbasid caliphate — roughly the period between the aforementioned Nawbakht and Abū Maʿshar — the mathematical disciplines, including but not limited to, astronomy and astrology, witnessed a tremendously dynamic increase of competence and complexity of subjects engaged among its often 'Iranian' practitioners. It was under the caliph al-Ma'mūn (813–833 CE/AH 198–218) — for whatever motives a great patron of secular learning — that the eponym of the third key term in the title of this presentation, *algorism*, was active; Abū ʿAbdallāh Muḥammad b. Mūsā al-Khwārizmī[35] was to lend his by-name, denoting a real or ascribed affliliation to Khwarezm, the ancient riverine oasis along the lower Oxus,[36] to an entire subsystem of mathematics[37] — it is superfluous to add that this perspective of his achievement, taking the Latin reception of his treatise on 'Computing with Indian numbers' as vanishing point, grossly distorts his actual position in the history of 'Arabic' mathematics and learning in general.

Not unusual in his environment and time, hardly any biographical information beyond the mentioned period and locale of his activity, Baghdad, is available on al-Khwārizmī, especially including his purported origin from the province of Khwarezm. The first two Abbasid centuries saw a notable brain drain, frequently effected by slave trade, from outlying regions to the centre, and increasingly, the capital Baghdad, itself. However, al-Khwārizmī's multifarious literary production establishes him as a major figure in the formative stages of 'Islamic' — as above, in the sense of Hodgson's *Islamicate* — science and learning. In his own writings in mathematics proper, astronomy and astrology, he displays the same uncertain Graeco-Indian eclecticism which marked Islamic science generally for the better part of the ninth century CE. The long shadow he cast on the evolution of these fields in medieval Europe may have tended somewhat to obscure the fact that their progress in the lands of Islam soon rendered his works obsolete — as mirrored by their fragmentary preservation. Neither his above-mentioned treatise on 'Indian arithmetic' nor his astronomical textbook with tables (*zīj*), of similar impact in medieval Europe, have survived in Arabic — by contrast, his seminal work on *algebra* did.[38] To the Latins, it did not only transmit its subject matter but also its name, although the Latin translators came up with an equivalent.[39]

It will, hopefully, not be taken amiss if in conclusion, we restate our previous protestations of a more comprehensive view of 'Iranian science' than here indicated by a few examples; thus the foregoing observations on the mathematical disciplines are categorically not to suggest that the period between al-Khwārizmī and al-Bīrūnī were void of outstanding scholars of variously Iranian connection. The contrary is true, whether or not their place of residence and work was in Iran and whether or not their given names or by-names proclaim an Iranian connection; from the host of names that come to mind, just a few may be mentioned to illustrate the point, such as an-Nayrīzī, Abū Jaʿfar al-Khāzin, al-Farghānī, ʿAbd ar-Raḥmān aṣ-Ṣūfī, al-Khujandī, Abū'l-Wafā' al-Būzjānī, as-Sijzī, Abū Naṣr b. ʿIrāq.[40]

The three terms figuring in the title of this broad sketch — oranges, quiddities, and algorisms — have been used as focussing lenses in order to highlight the contribution of 'Iran' — in a very broad sense — to the veritable plethora of science and learning in pre-Turkish Islam (until the mid-eleventh century CE). The linguistic garb of the relevant literary manifestations can in no way serve as an index of 'Iranianness', given that numerous Arabic texts closely reflect Iranian traditions whereas conversely, Persian writings may be little more than translations from Arabic. The question of continuity and survival of Iranian traditions from before Islam does not admit of facile generalisations; answers will be contingent on close case-by-case scrutiny and, at any rate, will vary by discipline, place and time.

Notes:

1. Cockayne 1864-1866.
2. On Ibrāhīm ibn Ya'qūb aṭ-Ṭarṭūshī see Buisseret 2007: 402-403.
3. Perhaps sericulture was the most outstanding example.
4. Cf. *arancia* in Italian.
5. Generally on medicine cf. Pormann and Savage-Smith 2007.
6. Cf. Richter-Bernburg 1999: 139-167. Also *idem* 2000: 299-317 and *idem* 1998: 219-233.
7. The select following ought not to be overlooked given limited space or due to their somewhat lesser renown: 'Alī ibn Sahl Rabban aṭ-Ṭabarī (b. c. 780 CE/AH 165, still active c. 855 CE/AH 240); Aḥmad b. Muḥammad aṭ-Ṭabarī at-Turunjī (fl. c. 970 CE/AH 360); Abū Sahl al-Masīḥī (c. 970 CE/AH 360 – 1010 CE/AH 401), and among writers of Persian (see below) Abū Bakr Rabī' ibn Aḥmad al-Akhawaynī (fl. mid-10th century CE.)
8. The above-mentioned Abū Bakr al-Akhawaynī al-Bukhārī, a student of ar-Rāzī's one generation removed was the first to compose a medical textbook in Persian, *Hedāyato l-mota'allemīn fī t-ṭibb*. In 980 CE/AH 370 Ḥakīm Maysarī completed his *Dāneshnāme*, a medical manual in c. 4,500 epic couplets.
9. Cf. Richter-Bernburg 1999: 147-149.
10. Achena 1987: 99-104.
11. Reference is to *Ẕakhīre-ye Khwārezmshāhī* by Esmā'īl Jorjānī; see Richter-Bernburg 1978: 2-8; nevertheless, as formulated in the preface to his Arabic translation of *Ẕakhīre*, this very Jorjānī's attitude to Persian appears to echo al-Bīrūnī's (on which further below); see Richter-Bernburg 1974: 55-64, esp. 60.
12. Cf. Richter-Bernburg 1974: 60-61.
13. *Ibid.* especially pp. 59-60; cf. Bīrūnī, ed. and tr. Strohmaier 2002: 32f. On al-Bīrūnī generally see *ibid.* 9-31; Bosworth *et al.* 1989: 274-287; Kennedy 1970: 147-158.
14. Minorsky 1953: 110-116.
15. See Goodman 1994: 474-477; Richter-Bernburg 2005: 299-308; *id*em 1994: 377-392.
16. Richter-Bernburg 2008: 119-130, esp. 127f.
17. al-Rāzī, tr. Greenhill 1848.
18. Micheau 1994: 1-15.
19. Mahdi *et al.* 1987: 66-110, esp. 66-70.
20. See the pertinent contributions in Burnett and Jacquart 1994.
21. Burnett 2000: 1-78 [pp. 20-78: Appendices], esp. 6-8, 22, 26, 28, 38.
22. Musallam 1987: 94-99.
23. Weisser 1987: 107-110.
24. Burnett 2005: 370-404; Zonta 2006: 89-105.
25. van Riet 1972; Fidora 2004: 10-26, esp. 22ff.
26. Cf. Janssens 2006 esp. nos. XIV-XVII; Janssens and de Smet 2002.
27. See 'quiddity' in *OED* at http://dictionary.oed.com/entrance.dtl.
28. Endreß 1992: 19, 21; Martin 1984: 103, n. 7.
29. With reference to al-Bīrūnī's own words, Kennedy is able to refute the transmitted date of al-Bīrūnī's death, 13 December 1048, and to postpone it to 1050 at least as in Kennedy 1970: 151.
30. Pingree *et al.* 1987: 858–871, esp. 859, 869; cf. Fahd 1993: 105-108.

31. It was Tammūz 23, 1074 Seleucid ('Anno Alexandri'), equivalent to July 30, 762 CE; see al-Bīrūnī, tr. Sachau 1879: 262, 29-40; also the Arabic edn. of 1878: 270, 11-17; cf. Wiedemann 1912: 1-40, esp. 19, n. 7 (references *inter alia* to al-Ya'qūbī, tr. Wiet 1937:11f.).
32. Massignon 1992: 1043-1044; Sezgin 1979: 100f.
33. Saliba 1992: 45-67.
34. Abu Ma'shar, ed. & tr. Yamamoto and Burnett 2000: I, xiii-xxii.
35. Vernet 1978: 1070-1071; Sezgin 1974: 228-241, *idem* 1978: 140-143, *idem* 1979: 128f., *idem* 2000: 86f., 92; Toomer 1973: 358-365.
36. Matthew Arnold's *Chorasmian waste* — in turn echoing Shelley's classical borrowing of *the lone Chorasmian shore* — surrounded the arable land next to the banks of the Āmū Daryā (see *OED* at http://dictionary.oed.com/entrance.dtl). Alas, it has since encroached on and swallowed up, large tracts formerly under cultivation as a result of irresponsible wholesale depletion of water resources in the Soviet era.
37. Initially just denoting the Indian place-value system of nine figures — with or without *zero* — *algorism* and its later derivative, *algorithm* (resulting from contamination with Greek ἀριθμός, 'number') eventually acquired meanings that in the computer age propelled *algorithm* into fairly widespread use; see *OED* (as in note 36). The first attestation of the term in Middle English, c. 1230, postdates by just a century John of Seville's Latin version of an adaptation of al-Khwārizmī's original; there, his *nisba* still properly functions as a personal name: *Incipit Arismethica Alchoarismi. Dixit alchoarizmi*; see al-Khwārizmī, ed. and tr. Folkerts and Kunitzsch 1997: 21 but cf. *ibid.* v, 8-10, 13-18; also al-Khwārizmī, ed. Allard 1992. On the transmission of the Indian numerals see Kunitzsch 2003: 3-21.
38. Cf. Rashed, tr. Armstrong 1994: 8-21 (revised from French original, 1984).
39. *Al-jabr wa-l-muqābala* ('setting straight and balancing') was transcribed in the heading ('Liber Algebre et almuchabolae'), but in the text rendered into *restauratio et oppositio*; see Hughes 1989: 29.
40. Sezgin, see above n. 35.

6

The Cross and the Lotus:

The Armenian Miscellany *Patmut'iwn płnjē k'ałak'i* ('History of the City of Brass') On the Periphery of the Iranian *Oikoumene*

James R. Russell
(Harvard University, Cambridge MA)

Persian, literature as a didactic tool, a source of common reference in discourse, an embellishment of the art of living speech, is as central to the idea of Iran as Chaucer, Shakespeare, Austen, and Dickens are to the idea of England. Every morning, in September of 2000, a niece or nephew of my friend Professor Azhideh Moqaddam would stop on the way to school at my hotel in Tehran with a scrap of paper: an illuminated calligraphic verse of Sa'di or Hāfez they had memorised. I collected these; and they bind together the album (NP *muraqqa'*) of my cherished memories, of what I learned of Iranian life. They are — and we shall pursue this metaphor presently — part of the patched cloak of one's journey through life. Surely the glory of classical Persian literature had a native ancestor, but who is it? For most of the texts extant in Zoroastrian Book Pahlavi — the indigenous literature of the Sasanian era — are theological in content, with little pretense to aesthetic effect. They achieved the form in which they have come down to us only in the ninth century CE, three centuries after the end of the dynasty and at a point when it was obvious that, barring supernatural intervention, Iran was to turn decisively to Islam. The major works of this Middle Persian corpus deal directly with the *Avesta* and its *Zand*, elucidate points of Mazdean dogma and ritual, or engage in theological polemic — the Pahlavi *zand* of the Avestan *Yasna*, *Vispered* and *Videvdad*, the *Bundahišn* ['Creation', with an account of the confrontation of the primordial spirits of good and evil, followed by lists of the various creations], *Dēnkard* ['Acts of the Faith', sometimes described as a kind of *summa theologica*], *Dādestān ī dēnīg* ['Religious Judgment'], *Herbedestān* and *Nīrangestān* [treatises of sacerdotal training and practice, in a concise shorthand style], *Šāyest ne šāyest* ['Do and Don't'], *Mēnōg ī Xrad* ['The Spirit of Wisdom'], *Škand-gumānīg wizār* ['Doubt-dispelling Exposition', a polemic against other faiths]. The same priestly collection preserves various compositions attributed to the revered fourth-century high priest Ādurbād ī

Amahraspandān: *Čīdag andarz ī pōryōtkēšān* ['Select Counsels of the Ancient Sages', a catechism composed perhaps in response to such Christian texts as the Nicene Creed], prayers in the *Khordeh Avesta* such as the credal *Nām stāyišn* ['Praise by name is meet to Ohrmazd'], etc. A very few are episodes from the epic past of Zoroastrian Iran (*Ayādgār ī Zarērān* ['The Memorial of Zarer'], *Kārnāmag ī Ardešīr ī Pābagān* ['Acts of Ardeshir son of Papak']) or wisdom tales (*Draxt ī Asūrīg* ['The Assyrian Tree', a wisdom text in which the benefits to man of the date-palm and the goat are compared], *Jōišt ī Friyān* ['Youngest of the Friya Clan', in which a Mazdean youth defeats the sorcerer Akht, 'Vice' in a riddle contest]). And some deal with apocalyptic hopes (*Madan ī Varahrān ī Varzāvand* ['The Coming of Verethraghna the Thaumaturge', with vengeful predictions of the doom of Islam], *Zand ī Wahman Yasn*, *Ayādgār ī Jāmāspīg* ['The Memorial of Jamaspa', used by Parsis for divination], and probably in this category too the *Ardā Wīrāz Nāmag* ['The Book of Wiraz the Righteous', the account of an out-of-body visit to the infernal and heavenly realms, and thus a remote precursor of Dante]). The writings dealing with such secular topics as epistolary style (*Nāmag nibēsišnīh*), postprandial speeches (*Sūr saxwan*), chess (*Wizārišn ī čatrang*), and the pleasures of life at court (*Khusrō ud rēdag*), are few and concise. Even where they deal with eloquence, their style is cramped. Sasanian epigraphy is generally limited to political matters — as was the case with the Achaemenians, the Prophet Zarathustra himself is not mentioned once in the corpus, though Ohrmazd, the *yazata*s, and the sacred fire are. The several inscriptions of the third-century CE high priest Kirdēr, who checked the growth of Manichaeism in the empire, are an exception, and describe a visionary journey of the soul probably patterned on that of *Arda Wiraz*. And although the discovery a century ago of the Manichaean Middle Persian and Parthian corpus has enlarged our understanding of language and belief, the contribution of these texts to our knowledge of secular, artistic culture is, again, fairly meagre.[1]

Yet we know, notably from the catalogue (*Fihrist*) of the books in his father's shop composed by Ibn an-Nadīm — thank God for men of leisure — that there was a rich Sasanian secular literature alongside the writings of divines, and what we now possess seems to be, *grosso modo*, material that was deemed worthy of rescue and swiftly compiled for the purposes of survival of the Mazdean community in reduced circumstances. In rare cases, outside testimonia can be corroborated with surviving texts: Athenaeus in his *Deipnosophists* asserts that Persians paint scenes from the romance of Zariadris and Odatis in their temples — and the *Memorial of Zarēr*, mentioned above, exists in Pahlavi though its content is more religious than romantic. Other epic narratives in the lost Sasanian *Khwadāy nāmag* were the source from which Daqīqī drew material that Firdausi was in turn to incorporate into the *Shāhnāma*. But it is mainly to the translation activity of Ibn al-Muqaffa' and the *shu'ubīya* — the newly-converted Persian Muslims who committed themselves to preserving their old cultural treasures in a new tongue — that we owe the counsels attributed to king Khusrau Anushirvan and his vizier

Wuzurgmihr, the animal fables of the Indian *Panchatantra* that became, via Pahlavi transmission, the *Kalila wa Dimna*, the strands of tales threaded together in the story of the maiden Shahrizād that were to be assembled into the Arabic *One Thousand Nights and a Night*, and references to the lyrics of Barbād and other *gōsāns*. The mention of Indian storytelling reminds one that pre-Islamic Iranian literature was also a conduit for Buddhist texts: through Manichaean and Persian translations the teaching of the life of the Buddha and the *bodhisattva* doctrine outlined in the *Lalitavistara* became Christianized in the Georgian *Balavariani* and then through the Greek *Barlaam and Ioasaph* (falsely attributed to John Damascenus) was diffused through the European literatures.[2] The subsequent history of this text alone demonstrates the importance of this Silk Road of the intellect, as it were, to the fortunes of mankind: Leo Tolstoy in his *Ispoved'* ('Confession') avows that a parable in the book inspired him to turn away from wealth and worldly vanity and to craft the theory of non-violence; and Mahatma Gandhi and, following him, the Rev. Dr. Martin Luther King put the theory into practice.

Though the Persian-speaking centre was nearly always the core of power, one must look also to the regions upon which political history imposes the somewhat misleading but still useful designation 'peripheral Iran'— one might call it also, and more equitably, the Iranian *oikoumene* — to acquire a fuller picture of the literary heritage that was carried over into the Islamic period and to appreciate the rich, cosmopolitan diversity that informed it. Though my teacher Professor Nicholas Sims-Williams once opined that a word is worth a thousand pictures, I would like to approach my task beginning, at least, with pictures — the frescoes found in homes of Sogdian Panjikant, most of which date from the mid-eighth century CE, that is, shortly after the Arab conquest of the region.

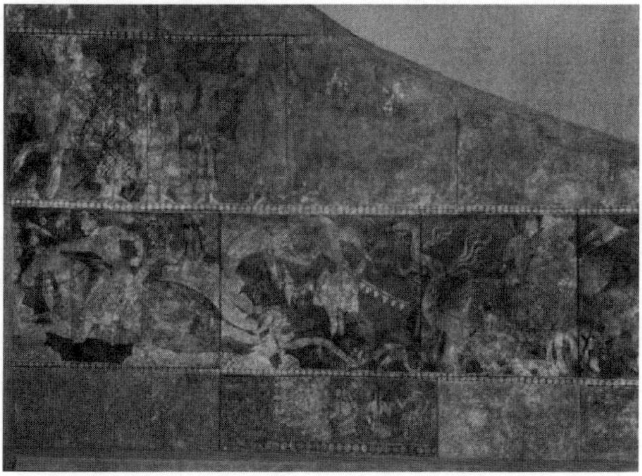

Fig. 1 – Panjikant frescoes, Sogd, c. 8th century; Muraqqa', Iran and Central Asia, c. late 14th century; Church of the Holy Cross, south elevation, Alt'amar, Vaspurakan, Armenia, 920 CE.

These are well known from the studies of the late Boris Marshak and others; so a brief survey of significant points should suffice. They were done by painters who executed also performance scrolls; and from written captions it would seem reciters of epics, fables, and romances entertained the master of the house and his guests much as the *Shāhnāma-khān* (a reader of the 'Book of Kings') does in a Tehran *qahva-khāna* (lit. 'coffee-house', actually a restaurant serving tea) to this day, gesturing to the pictures and adding interactive commentary to his text to involve the audience. The frescoes are in vertical registers; and when there are three, the order of subjects from the top down is divine, heroic, and human. The subjects are drawn from the same array of texts we have seen that are sparsely attested in Pahlavi but abundantly, in Arabic and New Persian: the exploits of Rostam the Saka, the *Panchatantra* and the fables of Aesop, and other sources such as local tales: indeed, in Marshak's words, 'we find illustrations to a whole library of the secular books so poorly represented among Sogdian and other Middle Iranian literary texts which have come down to us.'[3] The frescoes, while expensive, did not belong to royalty; rather, they suggest upward mobility and imitation by a mercantile class. Accordingly, a setting of travel thematically unifies many pictures of didactic character.[4] Presumably allegories about the acquisition of wisdom couched in the narrative framework of travel existed in other media used for social entertainment, such as painted scrolls and books: one argued long ago for the authenticity of a Sogdian bas-relief with a Zoroastrian funerary scene of the Northern Qi period in China that probably also tells the life story of a traveling merchant; since then, several other such narrative bas-reliefs have come to light.[5]

Another important feature of the Panjikant frescoes is their eclecticism: Rostam rubs shoulders, almost literally, with fictional characters from perhaps as far away as Rome — if indeed the scene of a child suckled by a wolf is not of more locally Turkic or Hyrcanian provenance. Translated into literary terms, what we deal with is a miscellany; so, while negotiating the way back from pictures to text, we may consider briefly the genre of the *muraqqa'*. This Arabic term, which referred originally to the heavily-patched cloak worn by Sufis, came to be applied to the Persian albums in which choice

Fig. 2 – Panjikant frescoes, Sogd, c. 8th century; Muraqqa', Iran and Central Asia, c. late 14th century; Church of the Holy Cross, south elevation, Alt'amar, Vaspurakan, Armenia, 920 CE.

samples of calligraphy, drawings, and paintings were compiled for noblemen. The purpose of these 'gatherings of like material' both the systematization of knowledge and the provision of edification: they came out of what David Roxburgh has characterised as 'a long and venerated tradition of making compilations for the purpose of giving advice.'[6] The pre-Islamic Iranian component is strong: the calligraphy album of Baysonghur, for instance, contains aphorisms attributed to the Sasanian kings Ardeshīr and Khusrau and the latter's vizier Wuzurgmihr, with the latter repeatedly quoted as saying '*adab* is the best legacy'.[7] This maxim, which one might easily pass over as a commonplace remark, deserves some attention, as it points to one of the main reasons why miscellanies of *moralia* were compiled and frescoes with manifold parallel scenes painted. *Paideia*, *farhang*, *adab*: the concept of civility of values and manners rooted in a general education in the humane classics, as Peter Brown demonstrated in his taut, brilliant work *Power and Persuasion in Late Antiquity*, was the invisible binding force of society, the unwritten law, the tacit constitution that enfranchised the holy man, the wise counsellor, the learned orator to speak fearlessly to the powerful and that ideally prevented the arbitrary abuse of power by the latter. The social and semantic distance, then, from the patched *khirqa* of the dervish to the sumptuous royal album of precious works of art, is not that great; for what better lesson could civility impress upon king and commoner than the human common denominator of the evanescence of wealth, the transience of condition, the inevitability of mortality? That lesson might be clearest in fables and tales of itinerant Sufis and merchants, but it resounds through epic as well: *Et in Arcadia ego*.

And now to Armenia. Imagining the rim of the shield of Aeneas, Virgil did not think of Homer's Ocean stream but of 'the Araxes that suffers no bridges', a stock phrase — Tacitus knows it, too — for in Roman eyes the riparian frontier of Armenia was that of Iran as well: more than the watery wastes beyond the Pillars of Hercules, the Araxes was the impassable *eschaton* of the Empire. From the East it is less clear whether Armenia was considered *Ērān* or *Anērān*; yet Armenian culture, with its Zoroastrian substratum and huge linguistic fund of Iranian loans, can be fruitfully be viewed as the Iranian *chrétienté* — the particular expression of an Iranised Christianity that might have arisen in the metropolis itself, had the gravitational pull of the temperate Mediterranean — of the Biblical, Greco-Roman, and Orthodox cultures — exceeded the fierce, hot winds of the Arabian desert. Armenia is on the western periphery of the *oikoumene*; Sogdia, on the eastern — and the two display some structural affinities. Power in Artaxiad and Arsacid Armenia was largely decentralized in the hands of the hereditary dynastic clans of the different mountainous cantons, designated by the Parthian loan *naxarar*; while the country's cities were points of international commerce. Yuri Slezkine in a recent monograph[8] introduced the categories of Mercurians and Apollonians to distinguish cosmopolitan peoples whose strength derives from the movement of goods and services and the exploitation and development of information technology from nations that maintain themselves on defined territories, are ruled by landed hierarchies rooted in an agricultural economy, and rely upon military might. The Sogdians developed a far-flung commercial diaspora that reached its apogee in the post-Sasanian era; in the Armenian case, the diasporan pattern does not reach its fullness until the Ottoman centuries. But in literature and the graphic arts we can observe parallel developments, *mutatis mutandis* for the Christianised Armenian forms, that speak for a cultural kinship across the *oikoumene*.

Canonical scenes of the Gospels dominate pictorial narrative, with the important exception of portrayals in bas relief on memorial *xač'k'ars* 'cross-stones' of the typically Iranian royal hunt, the triumph during which the mounted nobleman bears aloft the ring of *khwarənah* (Arm. *p'ark'*), and of course fighting and feasting (*razm* yields Arm. *ṙazm-ik*, 'warlike', and *pate-razm* 'war'; *bazm* is loaned into Arm. *bazmem* 'sit [for a feast]'). [9]

Fig. 3 – Panjikant frescoes, Sogd, c. 8th century; Muraqqa', Iran and Central Asia, c. late 14th century; Church of the Holy Cross, south elevation, Ałt'amar, Vaspurakan, Armenia, 920 CE.

The outer walls of the tenth-century church of the Holy Cross on Ałt'amar island are decorated with bands of narrative scenes in successive registers of bas relief; and at times the animals gambolling in the vine scroll may mock the serious deeds of kings and prophets below. (Such satire is common in book illumination elsewhere in Christendom, as Michel Camille showed in his *Image on the Edge* and other studies; and it is known on churches as well.) We may have here a parallel to the stacked, linear narratives of Panjikant; and since perambulations of churches were done in consecration and ritual in Armenia, the bas reliefs might not have been merely mute tales, but visual support to a verbal narrative, in a sacralised variant of the entertainments enjoyed by the rich Sogdian merchant and his guests at a wine party. In any event the Armenians called their minstrels by the loaned Iranian term *gusan* (it has been largely superseded by Arabic *ashugh* now); and one of them, Kostandin of Erznka (Tk. Erzıncan), was asked by his 'brethren' (apparently members of a *fuṭuwwa*-like order) to compose and sing an Armenian poem in the metre of the *Shāhnāma*, suggesting they had some knowledge of the epic in the Persian original. He obliged them, and the result is a fair emulation.[10]

The first Biblical verse St. Mesrop Maštoc' rendered into Armenian in the fifth century CE, employing the new alphabet he had devised, was *Čanač'el zimastut'iwnn ew zxrat, imanal zbans hančaroy*, 'To know wisdom and instruction; to perceive the words of understanding' (Prov. 1.1, KJV), with at least one Iranian loan, from *khrad* 'wisdom' — and the practice of compilation of miscellanies of *moralia* seems to go back very far. Although MSS. containing a fair proportion of the contents of the miscellany that became popular under the designation of its title story, *Patmut'iwn płnjē k'ałak'i* (*PPK*), go back to the sixteenth century, the separate texts comprising the collection are known directly and from references centuries earlier.[11] Many of these have been individually edited, and have been studied with reference to other secular works of the Classical and Middle Armenian corpus, particularly the *Alexander Romance*.[12] The stable *PPK* text was printed first at Constantinople in the 18th cent.; and after subsequent editions there and at Tiflis, with some subtractions and editions, the last publication seems to have been a translation into Western Modern Armenian printed at Constantinople after World War I. The contents of the Tiflis edition of 1857 are: 1. 'The History of the City of Brass, which is an example of this world' *(Patmut'iwn płnjē k'ałak'i or ē ōrinak ašxarhis*), 2. 'History concerning P'ahlul the king' (*Patmut'iwn yałags P'ahlul t'agaworin*), 3. 'Helpful counsels made by the poet king whose name is Nušrēvan' (*Xratk' ōgtakark' arareal banastełc t'agaworin oroy anunn ē Nušrēvan*), 4. 'Useful and helpful counsels that Xikar the Wise made' (*Xratk' pitanik' ew ōgtakark' zor arareal ē Xikaray imastnoy*), 5. 'History of the girl and the boy and their questions to each other' (*Patmut'iwn ałǰkan ew mankan ew harc'munk' noc'a ənd mimeans*), 6. 'Life and history of Alexianos the ascetic' (*Vark' ew patmut'iwn Alēk'sianosi čgnaworin*), 7. 'History of lord Yusik and his son Step'annos' (*Patmut'iwn tēr Yuskan ew ordwoy norin Step'annosin*), 8. 'Children's amusements' (*Zbōsank' tłayoc'*). Peter Schäfer suggested that one study the contents of variant MSS. by identifying macroforms, that is, large, shifting, but relatively stable units of text, composed of microforms, smaller blocks of tradition that appear in different places in different MSS. or in other works entirely as well.[13] That is a good general method for studying the *PPK*: all editions have the title story, but most do not have the *Life* St. Stephen of Artamet; many versions of the famous pan-Christian story of St. Alexis the voluntary pauper exist in Armenian prose and verse; the counsels of Anushirvan are found in translation elsewhere, as is the tale of king Bahlōl, who abandoned his throne to become a dervish; and the Armenian translation of *Aḥiqar*, which must date back to the fifth century, is an apocryphal text of the Bible. The chapter called 'Children's amusements' is in Tiflis and Constantinople editions of the nineteenth century and consists of two tables, the 36 letters of the Classical Armenian alphabet and the twelve signs of the Zodiac, each letter or sign accompanied by a sententious moral admonition.

The title story, of the City of Brass, is well known from the corpus of the *One Thousand Nights and a Night*; and of several extant Armenian versions the earliest translation, from Arabic, was made for David the Curopalate c. 1000 CE.[14] Though the contents of individual collections of the *PPK* shift, the City of Brass carries the message of the macroform, and the other texts echo it: life is a road with many illusory temptations and reversals of fortune, earthly rank is meaningless, the quest for glory is vain, and true wisdom is to be found in prayerful submission to God, penitence, and renunciation.

Fig. 4 – Patmut'iwn płnjē k'ałak'i, *Constantinople, 1803, frontispiece showing the travellers entering the City of Brass.*

In the story, the caliph dispatches a party to find the jars in which Solomon had imprisoned the *jinn*. They travel past ruined cities, as well as domes or pavilions (*kubba*), where they read inscriptions about the vanity of life or are swallowed up by lethal mirages. At the end of their quest, on the shore of the ocean, they receive the jars and return; but when casks are uncorked in the throne room and the *jinn* are released from their millennial captivity, all they have to say is 'Repentance, O Prophet of God.' The chastened ruler renounces his throne and assumes the patched cloak of the dervish. The story belongs in general to the type of speculation about the ends of the earth, the confinement by Alexander of the barbarous nations Gog and Magog, and maybe also to the Iranian cycle about the mythical fortress of Kang. In its prosimetric style, with brief stanzas of verse recapitulating the action of the prose narrative, it reminds one of the Armenian version of the *Alexander Romance*; but, more importantly, the printed text indicates different spoken parts. That is, we deal with a performance, and are reminded of the uses to which the frescoes of Panjikant were put.

The theme of life's transient and evanescent qualities, together with this form of narrative interrupted by verse, places the City of Brass in the specific genre of the Buddhist stories studied by Victor Mair of T'ang China called 'transformation texts'.[15] One may perhaps mention more specifically as a source, maybe the ultimate one, the parable of the Phantom City in the most important cluster of transformation texts of Mahayana Buddhism in East Asia, the Lotus Sutra of the Good Law (*Saddharmapuṇḍarīkasutra*): here, the Buddha creates an illusory town to provide rest for his traveling band, then erases it when it is time for them to move on.

Fig. 5 – Patmut'iwn płnjē k'ałak'i, *Constantinople, 1803; Parable of the Phantom City, Mogaoku, Dunhuang.*

The story was understood specifically as a reference to the 'voice-hearers' who 'conceive an idea of extinction and enter into what they believe to be nirvana,' though it is in fact only a station on the way.[16] It is possible this text was composed in Central Asia, that is, in the milieu of travelling merchants who spoke Iranian languages — and the appeal of its selection of metaphors should be obvious. In only altered form, it was to prove equally popular to Armenians of a similar social and economic position, thousands of miles away and for over a millennium into the future. The 1803 edition of *PPK*, Constantinople, has a woodcut frontispiece displaying the scene of the travelers approaching the City of Brass; and there is a rather similar narrative fresco depicting the same climactic moment, but from the parable of the Phantom City at Mogaoku, Dunhuang, at the Chinese end of the Silk Road.[17] In the Chinese painting the Phantom City contains a *stupa*, or domed reliquary monument; and perhaps rendering of ruins in the desert as *kubba*, 'domes', of the Arabic and

Armenian is a remote attempt to understand this.

What we have, then, in Christian Armenia, is a miscellany that endured for perhaps a millennium in popular culture, a *muraqqa‘* of *moralia* in which a Buddhist transformation tale that probably took shape in Iranian Central Asia rubs shoulders with the counsels of a Sasanian king, the tale of another monarch who became a Sufi, and the hagiographies of hermits from as close as Van and as far away as Rome. If my suggestion that the Lotus Sutra is the source of the main story is right, then we find similar illustrations of the narrative at both ends of the Silk Road, with ample evidence from Sogd in between and in the Armenian text itself that the story was enacted as interactive performance. And now vignettes of the cultural life of the vast Iranian *oikoumene* assume shape, sound, color: a festive gathering, the *gusan* with his lute, bright pictures on the wall, narrations of wisdom and epic, lyric and romance interspersed with improvisatory verses, interpolations of wit. From there, forward across dark abysms of time, emerge the *muraqqa‘* album, the lively frescoes of a Tehrani *qahva- khāna*, and Professor Moqaddam's nephew with a verse from a classical *Dīvān*.

The multiple programmes of Sogdian narrative frescoes, the vertical registers of the bas reliefs at Ałt‘amar, the Persian scrapbooks of *moralia* and art, and the miscellany of Armenian tales with its unifying thematic structure, all create a dense pattern of contacts between diverse people and concerns, in which *adab/farhang/paideia* discerns common features and forges fellow feeling. But these stacked and parallel narratives by virtue of their very structure create something else, too: a polyphony in the presentation of literary characters, one that is neither linear nor hieratic, with a din of different social, ethnic, and religious voices acting upon each other. The result, even in a book of didactic intent, remains negotiation and dialogue between characters, rather than unified and normative statement. And in this aspect of the storytelling of the larger Iranian world that made its way westwards, and combined with the narrative devices of the cultures it encountered, one may perhaps discern the beginnings of a literary technique in which different kinds of voices meet, subjecting cliché subjects to satirical regard and probing new psychological insights — the first stirrings of those literary strategies that Mikhail Bakhtin, in his investigations of the phenomenon of literary *heteroglossia*, was to plot from Rabelais' deployment of the carnivalesque to the poetics of Dostoyevsky — the embryo of that primary vehicle of modernity itself, the novel.

Still at risk of putting one too many patches on the cloak of the dervish, one offers in conclusion a smaller observation, on the term *muraqqa‘* itself, that word for album which originally meant scraps sewn together. At the Sasanian and Armenian Arsacid courts the royal counselor was called *(dar) andarzbed*, Arm., *handerjapet*. Arm. *han-derj* 'clothing', cf. Arm. *derjak*, NP *darzī*, 'tailor', derived from OIr. **ham-darz-* 'bind or load together',[18] is clearly the same as. MP and NP *andarz*, 'precept, advice': clothes and counsel both indicate the proper form in which to be seen and in which to act; and it is wisdom that binds people together. Should this extension of the metaphor of clothing to the imperial counsel seem far-fetched, one need but recall the observation by the Indo-Europeanist Joshua Katz that the words vespers, Rus. *večer* ('evening'), Arm. *gišer* ('night'), etc. all derive from the same base as vestment: dusk is when the Sun and sky don evening dress. So the books of instruction for nobles and merchants proceed from the *andarz* of proper court attire to what may be then a linguistic calque on the Persian term or a parallel semantic result: the *muraqqa'*, the patched cloak of the itinerant holy man entertaining, advising, guiding the enchanted reader past *stupa*s and ancient ruins, past the City of Brass to the sea.

Notes:

1. The best descriptive essay on the subject remains Boyce 1968: 31-66; see also the chapters on the various literatures of the Middle Iranian languages in Yarshater 1983: 1151-1258. Since then numerous Bactrian documents have been discovered and published by Nicholas Sims-Williams. Iranists have not devoted sufficient attention to the Armenian literature of the Sasanian era and later, where the Iranian content is important, particularly in the epic genre; but see the studies of this writer and of Nina Garsoïan (*infra*). This writer has discussed the literary and philosophical connections and influences of a number of Pahlavi works in articles: 'The Platonic Myth of Er, Armenian Ara, and Iranian Arda Viraz', 'The Sage in Ancient Iranian Literature', 'Kartir and Mani: a Shamanistic Model of their Conflict', 'The *Do'a-ye Nam Stayishn*', 'On Mysticism and Esotericism among the Zoroastrians', 'A Parthian *Bhagavad Gita* and its Echoes', and other studies reprinted in Russell, 2004.
2. See Abuladze 1962 and Lang, 1966.
3. Marshak 2002: 105.
4. In one of these, according to Marshak's interpretation, a merchant encounters the spirit of the sea. This is an Indian oikotype of the theme encountered as the Biblical story of Jephthah, and is attested in Manichaean literature. Marshak elsewhere refers to the kinship of these tales to the rich heritage of Russian folklore; and one is reminded in this instance of the numerous variants of the famous ballad (Rus. *bylina*) of the seafaring merchant Sadko, and his encounters with the spirit of the deep. The source of the story is a place strikingly different from other Russian towns but structurally very similar to Sogd: the socially fluid, politically independent trading city of Novgorod. As is well known, early medieval Russia had strong commercial and cultural connections to Iran; so it may be that the ballad of Sadko itself is of Indian origin and came to Russia *via* a Central Asian or Iranian intermediary version, as I have argued was the case for the *bylina* of Il'ya Muromets and the Nightingale-Robber (*solovei razboinik*) in Russell 2005: 77-139 also published in Russian in *Rossiya XXI* 4, 2006: 156-197. On Sadko, Novgorodian democracy, and the transmission to Rus' of material from the *Bundahišn* and 'Zurvanite' cosmogonic myth, see Russell, *forthcoming*.
5. See Russell, 'Zoroastrianism and the Northern Qi Panels,' lectures at Harvard, March 1994 and University of California (Berkeley), April 1994, and published in Russell 1997 and reprinted in Russell 2004: 1445-1450.
6. Roxburgh 2005: 63.
7. Roxburgh *loc. cit.*
8. Slezkine 2004; see particularly ch. 1, 'Mercury's Sandals: The Jews and Other Nomads'.
9. Most of these were in Karabagh and Nakhichevan; for a study of several see this writer in Russell 2001: 187-215 reprinted in Russell 2004: 1135-1163, In recent years, cameramen on the Iranian side of the unbridgeable Araxes have documented the destruction by the Azerbaijan authorities of perhaps twenty thousand monuments in the cemetery of Julfa alone; see Ayvazyan 2007.
10. See Russell 1987: 6-7.
11. Examples include Brit. Mus. Or. Ms. 6990 (Conybeare, *Catalogue*, p. 269): dated A.D. 1587. Contains songs of T'lkuranc'i; prayer; the City of Bronze; 'History of the rustic and the matter of the acre,' in most of which a girl asks a boy riddles; 'Question of Gregory the Illuminator', in which the patron saint of Armenia fasts in

church forty days, till an angel appears to inform him about the future, heaven, and hell; the history of king P'ahlul; the hymn 'Morning of Light', by St. Nersēs Šnorhali; prayers of Narekac'i; a hymn to St. Sergius; and spells to be written on paper and swallowed, or consumed with bread and cheese. Brit. Mus. Or. Ms. 4580 (*Cat.*, p. 277): The history of Alexander of Macedon; the City of Bronze; king P'ahlul; the History of the Boy and the Girl; the History of king Zarmanazan of Assyria and a sequel on Farman, by Yakob of Arckē; the History of Barlaam and Josaphat; the History of Aḥiqar 'History of the spawning and rearing of Mohammed, servant of the Antichrist, and his reign'; History of the Antichrist, attributed to Agathangelos; songs of Aṙak'el *vardapet*, the Rose and Nightingale, by Catholicos Grigoris Ałt'amarc'i, of Yovhannēs T'lkuṙanc'i, of exile; prayers; the ballad of Narek; and a ballad about Alexianos. Brit. Mus. Or. Ms. 4548 (*Cat.*, p. 287): The History of the Boy and Girl; the City of Bronze; king P'ahlul; Alexianos; Aḥiqar; Portents of different days according to the phases of the Moon; prayers; and Turkish recipes. Brit. Mus. Or. Ms. 2624 (*Cat.*, p. 281): The City of Bronze; the History of the Boy and the Girl.

12. See Simonyan 1989 and her monograph on the poems composed to accompany such prose texts in *eadem*, 1975. Armenuhi Srapyan edited two of the texts found in most PPK miscellanies for which see Srapyan 1983.
13. Discussed by Davila 2001: 7.
14. See Russell 1983: 250-261.
15. For a discussion of this aspect, see J.R. Russell, '*Zhizn' dorogi i doroga zhizni: otrazhenie odnoi metafory v zhivopisi i literature sredneaziatskikh kul'tur i armyanskogo srednevekov'ya*,' ['Life on the Road and the Road of Life: The Reflection of a Metaphor in the Painting and Literature of Central Asian Cultures and the Armenian Middle Ages'], in Nikonorov 2004: 292-294.
16. See Watson 1993: 117-142.
17. See Wang 2005: 112-114 and figs. 2.20 and 2.21.
18. Bailey 1979: 166-167; on the Arm. usage see Garsoïan 1989: 530.

7

What Happened to the Sasanian Hunt in Islamic Art?

Robert Hillenbrand
(University of Edinburgh)

The 400 years and more between the Arab conquest of Iran in 637 CE and the coming of the Seljuqs in 1055 is a quite remarkably dark age in Iranian art. In part, the grand political movements of this era were responsible. The centre of gravity in the Islamic world was never Iran in this period. It was Syria under the Umayyads, Iraq under the 'Abbasids, and then Egypt and the lands to the west under the Fatimids. And the arts seem to tell the same story, notwithstanding the peerless epigraphic wares of Khorasan and the figural pottery of Nishapur.

Part of the problem is that too little survives to permit a consistent pattern of production, style and iconography to emerge. Every new important piece that turns up is a surprise, and each one changes the picture. Particularly in the case of precious metalwork[1] and textiles,[2] the problems of patchy survival are exacerbated by disputed provenance, date and — thanks to illegal excavations — authenticity. Yet it is highly unlikely that such a sparse and dubious picture of this key period of almost half a millennium is correct.[3]

The papers published in this book have demonstrated, in many different ways, the strength of Iranian national sentiment[4] and sense of corporate identity in this seemingly dark age. The *Shāhnāma* underlines the rooted affection for Iran's ancient heritage, not least that of the Sasanians. Nor were those feelings confined to eastern Iran.[5] Indeed, it could be argued, at least on the basis of surviving monuments, that, especially in Parthian and Sasanian times, western Iran was culturally some way ahead of eastern Iran.[6] The impact of Buddhism also gave eastern Iran a cultural colouring not replicated to the west.[7] It was only from later Umayyad times, when Khorasan became the focus for disaffection with Syrian Arab rule, and indeed the seed-bed for the Abbasid revolution, that the ethnic, political and to some degree even religious opposition to the Islamic polity that had developed far to the west took shape.[8] Under the Samanids in particular, and specifically between the late ninth and the early twelfth centuries, a new Perso-Islamic culture took shape in the east; in the visual arts this process can most easily be traced in architecture.[9] Its other expressions are sufficiently well known, such as the growth of Persian national sentiment under the Tahirids, Saffarids and Samanids; the development of New Persian as its preferred literary vehicle; the galaxy of poets who flourished in the tenth and eleventh centuries in eastern Iran and whose preferred language was again New Persian; and the dawn of a golden age of scientific achievement, best personified by the Khwarazmian al-Biruni.[10]

To the west, under the Buyids and lesser dynasties like the Bawandids, Kakuyids and Ziyarids, the immediately pre-Islamic past was also celebrated — from titles[11] to coins,[12] from crowns[13] to thrones,[14] from literary revivals like *Vis u Ramin*[15] to the use of the Yazdigirdi solar calendar,[16] as well as in the long survival of Sasanian typologies in the coins of Tabaristan,[17] in the use of Pahlavi inscriptions alongside Arabic ones in the Caspian region,[18] and in the celebrations of such traditional Iranian festivals as Noruz and Mihragan. Nor should one forget that the espousal of Shi'ism could also be interpreted, at least in part, as an assertion of difference from the Sunni orthodoxy of the Abbasid caliphate.

So while Islam was in the ascendant in many ways, the pre-Islamic tradition was still full of sap. And that certainly applies to the visual arts. The passage of time brought a dulling of the memory; old forms acquired new meanings, as in the paradigmatic case of Taq-i Bustan, which was brought to romantic life by stories of Farhad and Shirin.[19] Provincialism, too, could distort forms and themes that were originally metropolitan. Moreover, the decay or the re-working of Sasanian forms co-existed with the creation of brand new ones. All this is to say, then, that early Islamic Iran witnessed many different accommodations between the old and the new.

Architecture is perhaps the only field in the visual arts where it is possible to piece together a reasonably connected story — even though there are still many gaps.[20] Take the way that a simple countryside fire temple or *chahar taq*, of which the one in Firuzabad is a standard example, could be turned into a mosque simply by blocking off the opening nearest the *qibla* so as to make a mosque out of it, as the case of the *chahr taq* at Yazd-i Khast shows.[21] It is equally instructive to see how that small-scale, slimmed-down formula of a dome set on a square chamber with four axial openings could be transformed, by little more than a process of enlargement, into one of the great monumental Seljuq domed chambers like that of the Gulpaygan mosque. The process could equally well work in reverse. Thus the archetypal, iconic Sasanian palatial structure — the arch of Khusrau's palace at Ctesiphon, the Taq-i Kisra — could be reduced in scale, shorn of its lateral embellishments, with their uncertain use of Graeco-Roman classical vocabulary, and re-used in a new and now religious context as the great *qibla aivan* in so many of the Seljuq congregational mosques, as at Isfahan.[22] These examples — and they could easily be multiplied — show how Sasanian forms provided a launching pad for creating buildings of a totally different purpose and, eventually, of significantly different form.

All this is by way of preamble. The Sasanian hunt is depicted at its grandest and most ceremonious on one flank of the great grotto at Taq-i Bustan.[23] It is set in a huge game preserve (which helps to explain the amount and variety of game in Sasanian hunting images and their Islamic descendants), madly stampeding animals, an orchestra of musicians, serried rows of court ladies to watch the fun, grooms and elephants to clean up the carnage, and of course the star of the show himself, the shah, shown twice for good measure and larger than anyone else so that you cannot miss him. This scene, carved and painted in the late sixth century CE, takes place on a huge canvas — an entire wall of a mighty man-made grotto.

Fig. 1 – Taq-i Bustan: hunting scene (after Ghirshman 1962: pl.236).

But this same theme was enthusiastically developed by the Sasanians on a much smaller scale, especially in metalwork.[24] In this medium court artists created an arresting, propagandistic and increasingly streamlined, indeed iconic, image of the serene, dauntless, ever-victorious monarch, dressed in full fig and taking on the most ferocious beasts single-handed and at close quarters. As frequent find from sites far to the north of Iran, in the lands of the steppe nomads show, these dishes travelled as silent ambassadors and reminders of the supreme power of the Sasanian kings well beyond the Iranian sphere. But then came the Arabs and the humiliatingly rapid collapse of this apparently invulnerable monarchy. And political collapse ushered in a certain diminution, even dissolution, of the triumphant visual vocabulary of the royal hunter.

This seems to be the historical context for the textile which is at the heart of this paper. It is a fragmentary silk now in the church of Sant' Ambrogio in Milan which is part of a sequence of four very closely connected but not identical versions of the same theme. In its complete form, as preserved in Cologne, it has a repeat pattern of two affronted horsemen shooting their prey.[25] None of the four versions is dated, though the presence of the Milan piece on an altar in Sant' Ambrogio gives a *terminus post quem* of 835 CE. The textile was used to cover the inner faces of the gold altar made by a certain Volvinus in that church. Such a privileged setting clearly indicates that this textile was highly prized despite its fragmentary state.

Fig. 2 – Silk from Sant' Ambrogio, Milan (after Vollbach 1969: pl. 46).

Similarly, the almost identical textile in Prague forms part of the binding of a ninth-century Gospel book. Above all, though, in a field which is notoriously devoid of all but a very few fixed points in the matter of absolute dating — a field, it is worth repeating, in which dating and provenance are alike insecure, and where scores of pieces (especially transitional proto-Sasanian or early Islamic ones) are removed from the scholarly discussion because their authenticity is suspect — this proof that the Milan textile dates before 835 CE is especially precious. Its provenance, however, remains unknown. The costume details have suggested Syrian workmanship to some, but with the reservation that the workshop itself was Iranian.[26] This is certainly a working hypothesis, but it could be regarded as fudging the issue. Of course it is perfectly possible that a craftsman from one country — more, from one culture

— should work in another. But such a theory sidesteps the real problem, which is how to explain the co-existence in one object of different figural, iconographic and even religious traditions. Better, surely, to interpret such pieces — especially since they are numerous — as documents of a transitional period when artists were modifying inherited traditions by injecting new ideas, motifs, meanings and ways of seeing. In the case of the Milan textile, there can be no doubt that the scene illustrates a debased Sasanian iconography, and that is what constitutes its interest so far as this paper is concerned.

The Milan fragment shows two right halves (not matching halves) of the silk, and in its present state this half-image corresponds with tolerable exactness to a familiar type of Sasanian hunting image, usually encountered on silverware, in which the princely archer slews round in the saddle to loose a shaft at a rearing lion which menaces him.[27] The Parthian shot, as this pose is traditionally called,[28] thus has a powerful inbuilt tension, with the horse galloping in one direction, away from danger, while the rider, twisted in the saddle, courageously confronts that danger. The pose is the essence of drama. It also reflects the actual practice of the hunt — and of war. As a piece of design, too, such a combination of Parthian shot and menacing beast integrates the two opposing directions in an admirably self-contained unit ideally suited to the roundel form.

The fact that versions of this particular design, with widely differing colour schemes, survive in Prague, Cologne, Milan and St Calais (between Tours and Chartres) make it one of the most widespread compositions of the early Middle Ages, comparable in popularity, say, to the charioteer or quadriga silks.[29]

Fig. 3 – Reconstruction of the Milan silk (after Ierusalimskaja and Borkopp 1996: pl. on page 13).

It is now time to take a more general look at what is happening in this silk textile. This is a textile, we must remember, that survives only in a severely cut-down form. It is therefore important to try to reconstruct its original impact, and the dark blue version in Cologne, being more fully preserved, provides a better basis for this to be done, helped by the reconstruction published by Ierusalimskaja and

Borkopp.[30] If one imagines a textile of substantially larger size where this same design is repeated many times, it will become plain that its multiple roundels are disposed in serried horizontal, vertical and diagonal rows, depending on how one looks at them, and they themselves assert continually confusing and contradictory directions. Nor is this all. It is not merely a matter of overall impact, but of the effect at closer range, that is to say when one focuses on a single roundel. This particular textile — whether it was originally intended to serve as a curtain, a wall hanging or a garment — was so overloaded with detail that the main theme had to fight hard, and rather unavailingly, in its attempt to establish visual dominance. The mounted archer is merely one detail among many. There is simply too much to be taken in at first or even second glance. One detail after another, important or trivial, clamours for attention. It is indeed a classic case of the celebrated Islamic *horror vacui.* And on the micro as on the macro scale it is the sudden changes of direction that bewilder the viewer. This would be most true if the textile were part of a garment. When the wearer of such a robe moved, this decoration would quickly become a mere blur.

Yet this textile in Milan, and especially its Sasanian antecedents, cannot be fully understood without a closer look at how the theme of the hunt was interpreted in this very same medium of textiles, first to the west of Iran, then in the Iranian sphere itself, and finally to the east. This should establish the basic visual language on which the Milan textile depends, no matter how far it departs from these inherited norms.

First, then, the west, which in this context does not mean western Europe but the lands of Byzantium, Syria and Egypt. Roundels from sixth century Coptic Egypt clearly betray a vulgarisation of more complex models with their indifference to scale, their caricatured doll-like figures, frozen gestures and jerky rhythms.[31]

Fig. 4 – Coptic decorative roundel with two horsemen, 6th century CE (after Vollbach 1969: pl. 34).

In such textiles, which are not of silk, but of wool on linen, and therefore aimed at a less wealthy clientele, the notion of an actual hunt has almost disappeared — indeed, some of the animals are literally only half there. The plethora of detail, some of it only marginally relevant, also takes away the urgency of the event, and it is hard to take seriously the toy weapons that they brandish. Sometimes the hunting scene is still further diminished by being demoted to a surround for another scene altogether, such as Samson grappling with a lion.[32]

Much more serious competition comes from a solemn hieratic Byzantine image of two emperors on a lion hunt.[33] Movement has slowed to a standstill

Fig. 5 – Medallion with an emperor on a lion-hunt, perhaps 8th century CE, Mozac (after Vollbach 1969: pl. 55).

and while hunting dogs frisk about nuzzling their hind legs the lions are, it seems, obligingly trotting up to swallow the spears pointed with casual negligence in their direction by the gorgeously apparelled emperor. These are again a pair, and they stare out at us with a pointed disengagement from the business at hand. But for all the lifelessness of the scene — it makes a solemn ritual of the hunt — the artist has taken extreme care to dispose his figures to maximum advantage, spotlighting them against a plain dark ground and sparing no effort in decorating emperors, horses and lions like Christmas trees. Here we see the quintessential Byzantine severity and formal ceremony in its most heightened form. This textile has the added advantage of at least a clear *terminus post quem* dating of 761 when it was donated to St Calmin in Mozac by Pippin the Short.

Other Byzantine silks continue this theme of matched pairs of hunters, whether mounted or on foot, affronted or addorsed. All show a careful attention

Fig. 6 – Silk medallion with two horsemen, Maastricht (after Vollbach 1969: pl. 47).

to symmetry, to reasonably accurate proportional relationships, and to a due concentration on the key theme of hunting.[34] In most cases the theme is set in a roundel whose border comprises a series of vegetal or heart-shaped motifs. The link to late antique, early Christian and Byzantine wall paintings and floor mosaics is patent. Sometimes the design features a pair of hunters on foot in the upper level, each spearing a ferocious beast, and two addorsed hunters similarly occupied below. This simple counter-change is enough to ward off monotony, and indeed to add visual interest. In all these cases, despite the expensive material of the textile itself, the dress of the hunters — usually a short tunic — and the frequent lack of headdress leaves no doubt that they are not of princely rank.[35]

So much for the Christian Near East. What of the Iranian sphere itself? Here a couple of silks destroyed in World War II were widely accepted by those who had studied them as Iranian work, though their date remained uncertain. There is little doubt that if they turned up on the antiquities market today they would be incontinently dismissed as gross forgeries. This is a reminder of how little we still know of the norms and forms of early Islamic textiles in the Iranian world. In the case of these two textiles their ancient connections with church treasuries gave them an unimpeachable pedigree, so it is strange that they have been relatively neglected in recent scholarly literature, all the more since they are of major importance iconographically. As types they are far removed from any Byzantine silks, and their subject matter (as well as numerous details of their execution) are unmistakably Iranian. But their gross simplification of Sasanian crowns places them both firmly in the post-Sasanian era. That said, they draw on rather different sources for their iconography.

An obvious marker of a post-Sasanian date is the pillbox hat with an aerial worn by the hook-nosed and savagely determined king on the so-called Yazdigird silk — that identification is merely a name-tag.[36] This silk is associated with a papal gift of the eighth century to the monastery of Gerresheim in Germany, yet another reminder of how far from home such silks could travel, as we have already seen in the Mozac and Milan silks. In the so-called Yazdigird silk, the emphasis lies on elements derived, through an incalculable number of intermediate stages, from Achaemenid and even more ancient Near Eastern iconography. Hybrid monsters play a dominant role here, and it is the business of the king, like Darius and Xerxes before him, to subdue them. So, cheered on by the homun-culus in a nearby tree, he bridles the eagle-beaked griffin on which he rides and — turning in the saddle — holds in an iron grip the rearing horned and clawed monster that threatens him. In other words, he masters not only the natural but also the supernatural world. Again, the parallels with Achaemenid sculpture are instructive.[37] Such an image could scarcely be further removed from an Islamic world-view. These

Fig. 7 – So-called Yazdigird silk, Berlin (after von Falke 1913: pl. 105).

references to another world inhabited by mythical and symbolic creatures proliferate in Sasanian and early Islamic textiles alike. Lions couchant and regardant, and moufflon passant — these heraldic terms seem to fit their solemn, measured visual tone — fill the background in layered strips, a compositional device that recalls the friezes of pacing (and usually ferocious) animals so common in ancient Iranian art[38] and is so far removed from the standard medallion image of early medieval Iranian and Byzantine textiles. Some borrowing from another medium might explain this. Even the distinctive modelling of the animals' bodies by patches of colour seems to be a textile-based response to the strongly plastic internal modelling of animals in, say, Achaemenid sculpture. All in all, then, this silk wields with remarkable aplomb the visual language of ancient Iran even though it was probably designed at least a millennium later. The hunt has taken on mythical and religious overtones. As Ettinghausen has shown, this awareness of the distant past has parallels in early Islamic art in Iran,[39] and of course the Sasanians themselves had shown the way here in their numerous references to Achaemenid art and iconography and their pointed re-use of Achaemenid sites.

The Yazdigird silk owes very little to the classical world besides the minor solecism of the *clavi* or strips of embroidered cloth on the ruler's chest. The other clearly post-Sasanian silk, however, positively glories in such classical and Byzantine allusions, even though they are often woefully inaccurate, and this has led some to regard it as the work of artists in Constantinople.[40] They range from the use of an inhabited vine scroll for the border of this large medallion (87 cm in diameter) to the rigid frontality of the riders' poses, from the turriform element in their crowns, which recalls crowns worn by female classical personifications of cities, to their bare feet, and from their gallant but seriously flawed attempt to replicate imperial Byzantine costume to their long flowing hair, which is in marked contrast to the bunched hairstyle of Sasanian monarchs. Yet for all these borrowings from an alien tradition, this silk retains an essentially Sasanian flavour. Numerous details substantiate this, for example the affronted cockerels at 12 and 6 o'clock,

Fig. 8 – Bahram Gur silk (after Bréhier 1936: pl. LXXXVI).

the moufflon in the spandrels (both of them favoured creatures in Sasanian textiles), the pearled collars worn by the winged horses, and the diminutive lions bringing down horned ungulates immediately beneath the hindquarters of the winged horses. These are echoed by the larger lions each pouncing on their stag below. Each king grasps a branch of the central tree on which perches a bird of prey, perhaps an allusion to falconry. This again would point to a post-Sasanian date — the earliest visual references to the sport occur on Umayyad bronze coins[41] — as would the plethora of animals (no less than 14) that take up the lower half of the composition. Nevertheless, the designer has left just enough empty space, and has maintained a reasonably consistent scale, for the image to have room to breathe and to make sense.

The principal Sasanian feature is of course the subject matter itself. This depicts Bahram Gur snatching a lion cub from its enraged mother — five teats are carefully delineated — which leaps at his horse's hooves. It is beyond question that the doubling of the riders is in this case fatally inappropriate and destroys the credibility of the narrative.

All this leads naturally to the specific connection between the Milan textile and Bahram Gur, this most celebrated of Sasanian hunters, whether as prince or shah. As it happens, the key surviving literary texts which discuss the hunting feats of Bahram Gur all postdate this silk,[42] though it is entirely possible that the lost pre-Islamic *Khuday Namak*, a narrative of the Sasanian kings, dealt with this theme. The earliest of the surviving accounts is that of Ibn Qutaiba, writing in the tenth century, which deals in detail with the story of Bahram Gur and his slave girl Azada. She challenges him to perform three near-impossible feats: making a buck a doe, making a doe a buck, and transfixing a deer's foot and ear with a single arrow. He duly performs these tasks, whereupon she berates him for having the soul of a demon, not a man. He then pushes her off the camel they are riding, and tramples her to death. That is the last time he goes hunting with a woman. It is certainly the last time that she goes hunting with him. This became the defining episode illustrating Bahram's hunting skills, and as such it had a millennial lineage in Persian metalwork, pottery, miniature painting, carpets and other media. The story is retold in Firdausi's *Shāhnāma*, itself explicitly based on stories drawn from pre-Islamic sources, and in the *Haft Paikar*, or Seven Princesses, of Nizami, written around the year 1200. Yet these are not the only hunting feats of Bahram Gur. He was also a famed dragon-slayer; he snatched the royal crown from a throne to which two ferocious lions were tethered and which he first had to kill; we have seen how he taunted a furious lioness by stealing her cub; and he killed a lion and a gazelle with a single arrow. It is this latter feat that seems to be illustrated in the Milan textile. The embarrassment is that Bahram Gur seems to have had nothing to do with it; his attention has been deflected and is firmly engaged elsewhere. Iconographically, of course, this is a major solecism; and such solecisms are frequent in these post-Sasanian treatments of Sasanian themes.[43]

The theme of Bahram Gur and Azada turns up several times in the Sasanian period itself, in intaglios, in stucco and — most memorably — on a large silver-gilt dish.[44] This is sufficient evidence that a pre-Islamic iconographic tradition focusing on at least some of Bahram Gur's feats was well established,[45] and this in turn makes it likely enough that there were further, now lost, works of Sasanian art which depicted these other feats and could thus have served as a model for our textile. Moreover, a post-Sasanian textile in Augsburg also depicts Bahram Gur and Azada.[46] But, as we shall shortly see, the Milan textile contains ample proof that the image of the mounted hunter that it bears has already travelled a considerable distance from any putative Sasanian source.

It is now time to return to the Milan silk which is the core of this paper. It is a remarkable fact that this silk, whenever and wherever it was made, contrives in comprehensive fashion to squander the particular advantages of the Sasanian model on which it is based. It does so in various ways: duplication, omission, displacement and over-crowding. These are, as will soon appear, characteristic of non-Sasanian interpretations of Sasanian themes. It will be worth looking at each of them briefly in turn.

First, duplication. The presence of two horsemen instead of one and the fact that every detail of the design is duplicated in a symmetrical mirror image completely alters the impact of the composition. A single rider occupying the main portion of the design naturally exudes the dominance associated with royalty. Such a design is effective in symbolic terms and there are many examples on Sasanian textiles — though not of a horseman. That entire dimension is lost when the image is doubled. A speaking image is demoted to a decorative motif. Doubling was, of course, merely one option. A version of this theme in the Shoso-in at Nara,[47] datable to the rule of Shomu in the mid-eighth century at the latest and executed in a Japanese idiom (note the Chinese pictograph), is so designed that the hunter faces left and right in successive

Fig. 9 – Japanese silk of Sasanian inspiration (after Ghirshman 1962: pl. 445).

roundels. Moreover, the roundels are staggered in rows so that the same alternation operates on the vertical as well as the horizontal axis. This mirror effect is common in Sasanian textiles. One might add that, when the textile is seen as a whole, the effect of these successive subtle shifts in focus is to create a kind of continuous mobility and low-key variation which is very pleasing to the eye. In another Japanese version of this Sasanian theme[48] the medallion contains not one but four such horsemen, the top pair affronted though each is turned away from the other to shoot his prey, while the lower pair echoes this action but (absurdly enough) upside down.

Fig. 10 – Japanese silk of Sasanian inspiration (after Ghirshman 1962: pl. 444).

This theme of extra enrichment extends to the border itself, where the standard pearl roundel so typical of Sasanian textiles is itself surrounded by a further floral scrolling border. In the other Japanese textile previously mentioned the border is the simple pearl roundel alone, but there too an extra enrichment has been introduced, in that the field of the roundel border alternates regularly from green to blue. In a third Japanese version of the Sasanian hunt,[49] datable c. 750 CE, where the Chinese characters on the horses' flanks read "mountain" and 'happiness', four horsemen in superposed pairs, plus four rearing lions and a tree defining the central axis, are crammed into a single medallion with a mainly pearl roundel border. Thus the options open to craftsmen wishing to develop the theme of the Sasanian horseman were indeed wide.

Fig. 11 – Japanese silk of Sasanian inspiration (after Hayashi 1975: pl. 82).

The best evidence of omission, our second category, lies in the area behind the horses. The Parthian shot makes sense if the game is ferocious. Yet here the space behind the horses is taken up by nothing more formidable than a tree flanked by leaping hares, and each hunter's arrow points straight at one of these hares, at such close range moreover that he would be hard put to miss. No feats of skill here — and yet the whole purpose of the original iconography was to vaunt Bahram Gur's uncanny skill as an archer. The pose has therefore lost most of its purpose; no Sasanian *shāhanshāh* would deign to be depicted hunting game as small as this.[50] As for the costume of the rider and the treatment of the horse, the paraphernalia of royalty have been drastically reduced. The knotted tail, the acorn-shaped tassels, the ribbons streaming from the belt, the magnificent crown all these have been filtered out, and with them much of the heraldic and symbolic power of the image drains away.

Misplacement, our third category, is seen in the tableau beneath each of the riders. It depicts an onager being brought down by a lion in a pose which was already ancient in the Near East in Sasanian times, and indeed accurately reproduces the lion attacking the bull at Persepolis.[51] Yet this ancient astrological image, emblematic also of royal victory, is here put to an unexpected use as part of a narrative. An arrow lodged in each lion's shoulder identifies the scene as one of the hunting feats of the Sasanian king Bahram V (421–439 CE) later celebrated as Bahram Gur. He spied a lion savaging an onager and promptly shot an arrow which transfixed the pair of them and drove deep into the ground[52] — a detail overlooked here. Moreover, the rider is about to loosen a shaft in the opposite direction, so that there is no obvious connection between him and the wounded lion. This is not the only example of misplacement. Other animals fan out in front of the horse in approved Sasanian fashion; but, since the rider is looking in precisely the opposite direction, they too are so misplaced as to lose much of their meaning in this scene. One might add that the combination of several types of quarry is unusual though not unknown[53] in Sasanian hunting images. It is the norm for the ruler to concentrate on one type of quarry at a time. Yet another slight solecism is the visual connection between the animals below the horse and the defeated enemy trampled by the shah in many a Sasanian investiture or triumph.[54] Finally, the impact of the traditional Sasanian pearl roundel motif,[55] commonly used as the sole border design in Sasanian textiles,[56] is much reduced by the way that the pearl roundel has been swallowed up by a much more complex border design, and indeed has taken on some of the character of a bead-and-reel motif. Thus conflation is the essence of this design.

The last change to be considered is the addition of superfluous motifs. These are so plentiful that the design becomes overcrowded. The central tree is a case in point. Its principal function is to divide the picture space down the central axis. One may well doubt whether it has any deeper meaning than this. Around the riders a positive menagerie of creatures disport themselves — eagles, other birds, stags, hares and dogs.[57] Such little empty space as remains is filled with severed flowering branches, plants or even leaves. The Sasanian artists who created the great hunting scenes on the silver plates took good care that the background was left plain and thus did not allow it to compete with the principal image.

To summarise, then, the scene was in theory entirely suitable for a roundel composition. But the arrangement of the design here ensures that the ostensibly main subject has been relegated to a side-show, while the fact that the scene is shown twice means that it cannot really be interpreted as a historical record of Bahram's feat. The artist, as noted above, has signally failed to place the rider, lion and onager in rational rapport with each other. In this respect too, then, a potentially powerful theme has been drained of meaning. A specific theme has become a generic one. The influx of otiose detail has the same effect. So too has the absence of the identifying attributes of royalty — for example, the majestic Sasanian crown has given way to a winged cap with fluttering ribbons.

Most striking of all, a dominant single figure has been replaced by a crowded, busy scene. All that is on the debit side; on the credit side, however, is a degree of rhythm, symmetry and decorative pattern that the lost original probably never possessed.

What, in conclusion, does the Milan textile reveal about how a Sasanian aesthetic turned into an Islamic one? To put it briefly, the sense of awe has evaporated. Craftsmen had lost an easy familiarity with the *tout ensemble* of Sasanian royal iconography; they saw it as in a glass darkly. This was only to be expected once the major court or metropolitan manufactories, the natural repositories of centuries of experience and hence the guardians of what was fitting, had ceased to function. There was a random quality to what was remembered, and to how accurate the memories were.[58] Artists took what they could from the past, and tried to integrate it with their own vision. So there is a good deal of stuttering. But these were also images of royal majesty and power which proved surprisingly resilient, and which could triumph over numerous mistakes of detail and of balance.

Something else is at work here. As was only to be expected, these post-Sasanian pictorial textiles, being transitional, often have a foot in two camps. They look back to a world of isolated large-scale images which owe much of their impact to their absolute size and simplicity. But they also look forward to a world in which small-scale pattern played a much greater role, and where ornament was perceived as a busy overall covering of a surface. That is the world of late Umayyad carved stone and plaster, and of Samarra stucco. Figural art, in textiles as in other media, had to make some compromises to fit into that new aesthetic. The Milan textile, which is perhaps of Umayyad date, marks a moment when pattern was beginning to swallow up meaning but was itself still not yet under full control. Nor do inscriptions yet play a part in its design. Gradually over the next couple of centuries pattern, and with it the role of inscriptions, asserted itself with increasing force, and figural elements had to share the available space with these competitors. The St. Josse silk is a good example of this next stage of evolution. But it was not until the Seljuq period that a comfortable balance between abstract, vegetal or geometric ornament, epigraphy and figural elements was attained.

The time is ripe for a re-assessment of early Iranian Islamic textiles of pictorial character. The doubts cast on the authenticity of so much of this material by recent scholarship should not be allowed to obscure the fact that in European church treasuries there still exists a mass of pictorial post-Sasanian textiles whose authenticity is unimpeachable, with pedigrees stretching back sometimes a thousand years and more. Controlled excavations are gradually adding to this total. The textual references so meticulously assembled by Serjeant two generations ago provide ample literary evidence to indicate just how important and pervasive costly textiles were as markers of rank and wealth. These various groups of data now need to be re-assessed together with a view to developing an up-to-date synthesis that will restore these early Islamic Iranian textiles to their rightful position in the history of Iranian art.

Notes:

1. Atıl, Chase and Jett 1985, Appendix III.
2. Blair, Bloom and Wardwell 1992.
3. It is telling evidence of this scholarly neglect that the last attempt at an overview of Buyid art, and that a pretty short one, was published over fifty years ago in Kühnel 1956.
4. Stern 1971 represents an early attempt to tackle this problem.
5. The whole issue of eastern versus western Iran as the source for major cultural achievements was hotly debated in the earlier part of the last century. See Bartol'd 1922 conveniently summarized in Minorsky 1964: 61-63.
6. Herzfeld 1921: 119, 147, and 152, where he notes that the evidence of historical sources, surviving monuments, and references to vanished monuments all concur in suggesting that eastern Iran was culturally far behind western Iran in Parthian and Sasanian times.
7. Herzfeld 1921: 146; Melikian-Chirvani 1974; Melikian-Chirvani 1975.
8. Herzfeld 1921: 120.
9. Key monuments include a quartet of mausolea, every one of them a masterpiece — the tomb of the Samanids in Bukhara, the 'Arab-Ata mausoleum in Tim, the Gunbad-i Qabus and the tomb tower of Radkan West, all probably built within a single century and each very different from the next.
10. Herzfeld 1921: 120-121, 173-174. See also Chelkowski 1975: 1-168.
11. Madelung 1969; Richter-Bernburg 1980.
12. Such as the titles *Shāhanshāh* and its Arabic equivalent *Malik al-mulūk*, or hybrid titles like *al-Malik Shāhanshāh*, *al-Amīr Shāhanshāh* or *Shāhanshāh al-a'zam*. See Treadwell 2001: xxx-xxxii and xxxiv.
13. Particularly Bahrami 1952: pl. I/1a, 2a, 2b and 4a. On the medal depicted in pl. I/1a-b, see Atıl, Chase and Jett 1985: 267, where it is listed among works that "require further research to establish their provenance and date".
14. See Spuler 1952: 346 for the case of the golden throne made in direct imitation of Sasanian work by Mardawij b. Ziyar.
15. Gurgani 1972.
16. Van Berchem 1918: 104-106.
17. Walker 1941: 130-161 and pls. xxiii-xxvii.
18. Herzfeld 1932; Godard 1936: 112-114, 120; Herzfeld 1936: 78-81.
19. Soucek 1974.
20. The most up-to-date detailed survey of this material is to be found in Anisi 2007. For a brief conspectus of this material, see Hillenbrand 1985.
21. Smith 1940; Siroux 1947.
22. Grabar 1990: 91.
23. For the fullest account of all the reliefs see Fukai 1972 and 1984.
24. Erdmann 1936; Grabar 1967: 47-55; and Harper 1981: 40-98 and pls. 8-32, 37-38. Also see von Gall 1990 for the latest detailed survey of the theme.
25. Von Falke 1913: I, 70-74 and Abb. 69; Pierce and Tyler 1936 (the Prague silk); Volbach 1969: 101, pl. 46 for a colour illustration of the Milan fragment.
26. Ghirshman 1962: 235. The same reasoning would presumably apply to the other versions at Cologne, Prague and St Calais (Sarthe). Ettinghausen 1972: 38 believes that the Milan piece is probably Umayyad.
27. Harper 1981: pls. 14 and 37; Hayashi 1975: pl. 84.
28. Rostovtzeff 1943.

29. Volbach 1969: 88. It is worth noting Volbach's view that these four versions of the mounted hunter, like the quadriga fabric in Aachen, are "Byzantine work...more stylized and predominantly influenced by Persia".
30. Ierusalimskaja and Borkopp 1996: 13.
31. Volbach 1969: 57, and, for a colour illustration, pl. 34.
32. *Ibid.* pl. 35 for a colour illustration.
33. Bréhier 1936: 101 and pl. xc. He expresses doubts about the connection with Pippin the Short but gives no reason for doing so. Volbach 1969: 113-114, 118 regards this tradition as genuine. For a colour illustration, see Volbach 1969: pl. 55. Cf. von Falke 1913: II, 4-5.
34. E.g. the Maastricht silk, Balty *et al.* 1993: 115 to be supplemented by Volbach 1969: pl. 47.
35. E.g. Volbach 1969: pls. 50 and 59.
36. Von Falke 1913: 83-85 and pl. 105.
37. Curtis and Tallis 2005: pl. 42; 82, cat. nos. 41-42; 92-94, cat. nos. 66-74; 158-159, cat. no. 202; and 160, cat. no. 208. Cf. Ghirshman 1964: pls. 250-253.
38. As at Ziwiye, for example Diba 1965: figs 69-73b and 75-76.
39. Ettinghausen 1969.
40. Bréhier 1936: 99 and pl. lxxxvi; cf. von Falke 1913: I, 85-86.
41. Oddy 1991; cf. Allen 1980: 127-128.
42. See Ettinghausen 1979 for what follows.
43. Hillenbrand 2006.
44. Harper 1978: 48-50.
45. See also the ivory casket formerly in the Stoclet Collection in Brussels; Shalem 2004: 125, fig. 9.10.
46. Shalem 2004.
47. See Ghirshman 1962: pl. 445 for a colour illustration.
48. Hayashi 1975: pl. 13. For a very similar piece from the Horiyushi temple see von Falke 1913: I, fig. 111.
49. Hayashi 1975: pl. 82.
50. Harper 1981: *passim*; Harper 1978: *passim.*
51. Ghirshman 1964: pl. 240.
52. Tabari 1999: 85. This incident does not figure in the discussion of the iconography of Bahram Gur as given in Ettinghausen 1979.
53. Ghirshman 1962: fig. 247 — a plate which shows two gazelles, a moufflon and two bears.
54. Herrmann 1977: 90-93, 96 (plates illustrating six examples in all).
55. Meister 1970.
56. E.g. the boar's head textile from Astana in Ghirshman 1962: fig. 281. It was standard practice for such borders to include a different motif, such as a rosette or a square, at the four cardinal points; also, Balty *et al.* 1993: 136, fig. 131; 274; and 276.
57. The presence of dogs strengthens the case for a post-Sasanian dating. The frescoes of Qusair 'Amra in the Jordanian desert show a pack of hunting dogs. See Almagro *et al.* 1975: Láms. xxviiib and xxixa, b. By way of contrast, Sasanian hunting plates on the whole do not depict hunting dogs, though a solitary specimen occurs on the Ufa plate as in Fajans 1957: 65 and fig. 16.
58. An extreme case is a silk depicting a cavalier, which was found in the region of the Urals and is now in the museum at Tcheliabinsk. See Balty *et al.* 1993: 117, fig. 106.

Abbreviations

AJA	*American Journal of Archaeology*
AJSLL	*American Journal of Semitic Languages and Literatures*
AMI	*Archäologische Mitteilungen aus dem Iran*
AI	*Ars Islamica*
AO	*Ars Orientalis*
BEO	*Bulletin d'Études Orientales*
BIFO	*Bulletin de l'Institut français d'Archéologie orientale*
BSO[A]S	*Bulletin of the School of Oriental [and African] Studies*
CHIr	*The Cambridge History of Iran*
DSB	*Dictionary of Scientific Biography*
EW	*East and West*, n.s.
EI[1]	*Encyclopaedia of Islam*, 1st edn.
EI[2]	*Encyclopaedia of Islam,* 2nd edn.
EncIr	*Encyclopaedia Iranica*
HdO	*Handbuch der Orientalistik*
GAS	*Geschichte des arabischen Schrifttums*
IJMES	*International Journal of Middle Eastern Studies*
IFRI	*Institut français de recherche en Iran*
Isl.	*Der Islam*
JAOS	*Journal of the American Oriental Society*
Iran	*Journal of the British Institute of Persian Studies*
JIS	*Journal of Islamic Studies*
JNES	*Journal of Near Eastern Studies*
JRAS	*Journal of the Royal Asiatic Society*
JSS	*Journal of Semitic Studies*
KJV	*King James Version*
NC	*Numismatic Chronicle*
OED	*Oxford English Dictionary*
Prov.	*Book of Proverbs*
RSO	*Rivista degli Studi Orientali*
StIr	*Studia Iranica*
Survey	*A Survey of Persian Art from Prehistoric Times to the Present*
ZDMG	*Zeitschrift der deutschen morgenländischen Gesellschaft*

Bibliography

Abuladze, I. V. (1962) (ed.) *Balavariani: Mudrost' Balavara*, Tbilisi.

Achena, M. (1987). 'Avicenna xi: Persian Works', *EncIr* III: 99-104.

Allen, M. (1980). *Falconry in Arabia*, London.

Almagro, M., Caballero, L., Zozaya, J. and Almagro, A. (1975) *Qusayr 'Amra. Residencia y baños omeyas en el desierto de Jordania*, Madrid.

Amedroz, H. (1905). 'The Assumption of the Title Shāhānshāh by Buwayhid rulers', *NC* Series 4, 5: 393-399.

Anisi, A. (2007). *Early Islamic Architecture in Iran (637-1058)*. Unpublished PhD thesis, University of Edinburgh.

Atıl, E., Chase, W. T., and Jett, P. (1985). *Islamic Metalwork in the Freer Gallery of Art*, Washington DC.

Axworthy, M. (2008). *A History of Iran: Empire of the Mind*, New York.

Ayvazyan, A. (2007). *Jułayi korcanvac xač'k'areri simfonian*, Erevan.

al-Baladhuri (1863-66). (ed.) de Goeje, M., *Futūh al-buldān,* [*Liber expugnationis regionum* ...], 3 vols. in 1, Leiden.

al-Biruni (1878). (ed.) Sachau, C. E., *Chronologie orientalischer Völker*, Leipzig

— (1879). (transl.) Sachau, C. E., *al-Āthār al-bāqiya 'an al-qurūn al-khāliya* [*The chronology of ancient nations*], London.

— (2002). (transl. and ed.) Strohmaier, G., *In den Gärten der Wissenschaft*, Leipzig.

al-Bukhari (1965). (ed.) Matini, J., *Hidāyat al-muta'allimīn fī al-tibb*, Mashhad.

Bahrami, M. (1952). 'A Gold Medal in the Freer Gallery of Art', in Miles, G. C. (ed.), *Archaeologia Orientalia in Memoriam Ernst Herzfeld*, Locust Valley: 5-20.

Bailey, H. W. (1979). *Dictionary of Khotan Saka*, Cambridge.

Bartol'd, V. V. (1922). 'Vostochno-iranskii vopros', *Izvestiya Materialnoi Kulturi* II: 361-384.

Bayhaqi (1971). (ed.) Fayyad, 'A. A., *Tārīkh-i Mas'ūdī*, Mashhad.

Berchem, M. van (1918). 'Die Inschriften der Grabtürme', in Diez, E. (ed.), *Churasanische Baudenkmäler*, Berlin: 87-116.

Blachère, R. (1935). *Un poète arabe du IVe siècle de l'Hégire: Aboû-Tayyib al-Motanabbî* (*essai d'histoire littéraire*), Paris.

Bladel, K. van (forthcoming). 'The Bactrian Background of the Barmakids'.

Blair, S., Bloom, J. M. and Wardwell, A.E. (1992). 'Reevaluating the Date of the 'Buyid' Silks by Epigraphic and Radiocarbon Analysis', *AO* XXII: 1-41.

Blair, S. (1992). *The Monumental Inscriptions from Early Islamic Iran and Transoxiana*, Leiden.

Bosworth, C. E. (1968). *Sīstān under the Arabs: From the Islamic Conquest to the Rise of the Ṣaffārids (30-250/651-864)*, Rome.

— (1969). 'The Tāhirids and Arab culture', *JSS* 14: 47-54, 71. (Reprinted in Bosworth 1982a, no. II).
— (1973). 'The Heritage of Rulership in Early Islamic Iran and the Search for Dynastic Connections with the Past', *Iran* XI: 51-62. (Reprinted in Bosworth 1977, no. VII).
— (1986). 'Khurāsān', *EI*^{2} V: 55-59.
— (1975). 'The Ṭāhirids and Ṣaffārids', in Frye, R. N. (ed.), *CHIr* 4, Cambridge.
— (1977). *The Medieval history of Iran, Afghanistan and Central Asia*, Variorum Reprints, London.
— (1982a). 'Barīd', *EncIr* III: 797-798.
— (1982b). *Medieval Administration and Culture*, Variorum Reprints, London.
— (1982c): 'Asfār b. Šīrūya', *EncIr* II: 747-748.
— (1990). 'Mardāwīdj', *EI*^{2} VI: 539.
— (1994). *The History of the Saffarids of Sistan and the Maliks of Nimruz (247/861 to 949/1542-3)*, New York and Costa Mesa.
— (1996). *The New Islamic Dynasties: A Chronological and Genealogical Manual*, Edinburgh.
Bosworth, C. E. *et al.*, (1989). 'Abū Rayḥān Bīrūnī. i. Life', *EncIr* IV: 274-287.
Boyce, M. (1957). 'The Parthian *gōšān* and the Iranian minstrel tradition', *JRAS*: 10-45.
— (1968). 'Middle Persian Literature', in *HdO* I/IV/2, Leiden: 31-66.
Bréhier, L. (1936). *La sculpture et les arts mineurs byzantins*, Paris.
Buisseret, D. (2007). (ed.) *The Oxford Companion to World Exploration*, 2 vols., Oxford.
Bulliet, R. W. (1979). *Conversion to Islam in the Medieval Period: An Essay in Quantitative History*, Cambridge MA.
— (1994). *Islam: The View from the Edge*, New York.
— (2009). *Cotton, Climate, and Camels in Early Islamic Iran: A Moment in World History,* Columbia.
Bürgel, J. C. (1965). *Die Hofkorrespondenz 'Aḍud ad-Daulas und ihr Verhältnis zu anderen historischen Quellen der frühen Būyiden*, Wiesbaden.
Bürgel, J. C. and Mottahedeh, R. (1982). ' 'Ażod al-Dawla', *EncIr* III: 265-269.
Burnett, C. and Jacquart, D. (1994). *Constantine the African and 'Alī ibn al-'Abbās al-Mağūsī: the Pantegni and Related Texts, Studies in Ancient Medicine* 10, Leiden.
Burnett, C. (2000). 'Antioch as a Link between Arabic and Latin culture in the Twelfth and Thirteenth Centuries', in Draelants, I., Tihon, A. and van den Abeele, B. (eds.), *Occident et Proche-Orient: Contacts scientifiques au temps des Croisades*: *Actes ...1997*, Turnhout.
— (2005). 'Arabic into Latin: the Reception of Arabic Philosophy into Western Europe', in Adamson, P. and Taylor, R. (eds.), *The Cambridge Companion to Arabic Philosophy*, Cambridge.

Busse, H. (1975). 'Iran under the Būyids', in Frye, R. N. (ed.), *CHIr* 4, Cambridge.
Cahen, C. (1960). 'Buwayhids or Būyids', *EI*[2] I: 1350-1353.
Chelkowski, P. J. (1975). *The Scholar and the Saint: Studies in Commemoration of Abu'l-Rayhan al-Biruni and Jalal al-Din al-Rumi*, New York.
Cockayne, T. (1864-66) (ed.) *Leechdoms Wortcunning and Starcraft of Early England*, 3 vols., Rerum Britannicarum Mediiævi Scriptores 35, London.
Curtis, J. and Tallis, N. (2005). *Forgotten Empire: The World of Ancient Persia*, London.
Daniel, E. (2000). *The History of Iran*, Westport, CT.
Davila, J. R. (2001). *Descenders to the Chariot: The People behind the Hekhalot Literature*, Leiden.
Davis, D. (2004). *Sunset of Empire: Stories from the Shahnameh of Ferdowsi*, vol. 3, Washington DC.
— (2007). *Shahnameh: the Persian Book of Kings*, London and New York.
Diba, P. (1965). *Les trésors de l'Iran et le vase en or des Mannéens*, Paris.
Endreß, G. (1992). 'Die wissenschaftliche Literatur', in Fischer, W. and Gätje, H. (eds.), *Grundriß der arabischen Philologie III: Supplement*, Wiesbaden.
Erdmann, K. (1936). 'Die sasanidische Jagdschalen', *Jahrbuch der preussischen Kunstsammlungen* LVII: 193-231.
Ettinghausen, R. (1969). 'A Case of Traditionalism in Iranian Art', in Aslanapa, O. and Naumann, R. (eds.), *Forschungen zur Kunst Asiens: In Memoriam Kurt Erdmann*, Istanbul: 88-110.
— (1972). *From Byzantium to Sasanian Iran and the Islamic World*, Leiden.
— (1979). 'Bahram Gur's Hunting Feats or the Problem of Identification', *Iran* XVII: 25-31.
Fajans, S. (1957). 'Recent Russian Literature on Newly Found Middle Eastern Metal Vessels', *AO* II: 55-76.
Fahd, T. (1993). '(Aḥkām al-) Nudjūm', *EI*[2] VIII: 105-108.
Falke, O. von (1913). *Kunstgeschichte der Seidenweberei*, I-II, Berlin.
Fidora, A. (2004). 'Abraham Ibn Daūd [sic] und Dominicus Gundissalinus: Philosophie und religiöse Toleranz im Toledo des 12. Jahrhunderts', in Lutz-Bachmann, M. and Fidora, A. (eds.), *Juden, Christen und Muslime: Religionsdialoge im Mittelalter*, Darmstadt.
Frye, R. N. (1975). *The Golden Age of Persia: The Arabs in the East*, London.
— (1975a) (ed.), *CHIr* 4, *From the Arab Invasion to the Saljuqs* Cambridge.
Fukai, S., *et al.* (1972). *Taq-i Bustan* II, Tokyo.
— (1984). *Taq-i Bustan* IV, Tokyo.
Gall, H. von (1990). *Das Reiterkampfbild in der iranischen und iranisch beeinflußten Kunst parthischer und sasanidischer Zeit*, Teheraner Forschungen VI, Berlin.
Gardizi (1968). (ed.) Habibi, A. H., *Kitāb Zayn al-akhbār*, Tehran.

Garsoïan, N. G. (1989). *The Epic Histories Attributed to P'awstos Buzand (Buzandaran Patmut'iwnk')*, Harvard Armenian Texts and Studies 8, Cambridge, MA.
Garthwaite, G. (2005). *The Persians*, Hoboken.
Gascou, J. (1985). 'Les grands domaines, la cité et l'état en Égypt byzantine', *Travaux et mémoirs*: 1-90.
Gibb, H. A. R. (1953). 'The Social Significance of the Shu'ūbiyya', in *Studia Orientalia Ioanni Pedersen Septuagenario Dicata*, Copenhagen: 105-114. (Reprinted in *Studies on the Civilization of Islam*, Shaw, S. and Polk, W. (eds.), Boston 1962: 62-73).
Gibbon, E. (1844-45). *The Decline and Fall of the Roman Empire,* Halifax.
Goitein, S. D. (1968). 'The Origin of the Vizierate and its True Tharacter', in *Studies in Islamic History and Institutions*, Leiden: 168-196.
Ghirshman, R. (1962). *Iran: Parthians and Sassanians*, London.
— (1964). *The Art of Ancient Iran from its Origins to the Time of Alexander the Great*, New York.
Godard, A. (1936). 'Les tours de Ladjim et de Resget', *Āthār-è Irān* I/1, 109-121.
Goodman, L. E. (1994). 'al-Rāzī', *EI²* VIII:474-477.
Grabar, O. (1967). *Sasanian Silver: Late Antique and Early Mediaeval Arts of Luxury from Iran*, Ann Arbor.
— (1990). *The Great Mosque of Isfahan*, New York.
Gurgani (1972). (transl.) Morrison, G., *Vis and Ramin, Translated from the Persian of Fakhr ud-Din Gurgani*, New York and London.
Hämeen-Antilla, J. (2006). *The Last Pagans of Iraq: Ibn Wahshiyya and his Nabatean Agriculture*, Leiden.
Hardy, E. R. (1931). *The Large Estates of Byzantine Egypt*, New York.
Harper, P. (1978). *The Royal Hunter: Art of the Sasanian Empire*, New York.
— (with a technical study by P. Meyers). (1981). *Silver Vessels of the Sasanian Period* I, New York.
Hayashi, R. (1975). (transl.) Ricketts, R., *The Silk Road and the Shoso-in*, New York and Tokyo.
Herrmann, G. (1977). *The Iranian Revival*, Oxford.
Herzfeld, E. (1921). 'Khorasan: Denkmalsgeographische Studien zur Kulturgeschichte des Islam in Iran,' *Isl.* 11: 107–174.
— (1932). 'Postsasanidische Inschriften I — Mil i Radkan', *AMI* 4: 140-147.
— (1936). 'Arabische Inschriften aus Iran und Syrien', *AMI* 8: 78-102.
Hillenbrand, R. (1985). ' 'Abbasid Mosques in Iran', *RSO* LIX: 175-212.
— (2006). 'The Islamic Re-working of the Sasanian Heritage: Two Case Studies', in Baker, P. and Brend, B. (eds.), *Studies in Honour of Géza Fehérvári,* London: 1-14.
Hovannisian, R. and Sabagh, G. (1998) (eds.). *The Persian Presence in the Islamic World*, Cambridge.
Hughes, B. (1989). *Robert of Chester's Latin Translation of al-Khwārizmī's* al-Jabr, Wiesbaden.

Ibn al-Athir (1966). *Al-Kāmil fī al-tārīkh*, Beirut.
Ibn al-Hassul (1940) (ed.) al-'Azzawi, A. *Kitāb Tafdīl al-atrāk 'alā sā'ir al-ajnād*, Istanbul; (transl.) Yaltkaya, Ş. in *Belleten* 4: 33-34.
Ibn al-'Imad,. (1931-32). *Shadharāt al-dhahab fī akhbār man dhahab*, 8 vols., Cairo.
Ierusalimskaja, A. A. and Borkopp, B. (1996). *Von China nach Byzanz: frühmittelalterliche Seiden aus der Staatlichen Ermitage St. Petersburg*, München.
al-Jahiz (1948). (ed.) Harun, M., *al-Bayān wa al-tabyīn*, 4 vols., Beirut.
al-Jahshiyari (1938). (ed.) al-Saqqa', M. *et al.*, *Kitāb al-Wuzarā'*, Cairo.
Janssens, J. and de Smet, D. (2002). *Avicenna and His Heritage*, Leuven.
Janssens, J. (2006). *Ibn Sīnā and His Influence on the Arabic and Latin World*, Aldershot.
Jawzi, Ibn (1938-40). *al-Muntazam fī tārīkh al-mulūk wa-al-umam*, Hyderabad.
al-Khwarizmi (1992) (ed.) Allard, A., *Le Calcul indien (Algorismus)*, Paris.
— (1997). (transl. and ed.) Folkerts, M. (with the co-operation of P. Kunitzsch), *Die älteste lateinische Schrift über das indische Rechnen nach al-Hwārizmī*, München.
Kennedy, E. S. 'al-Bīrūnī', in Gillispie, C. (ed.), *DSB* II: 147-158.
Khaldun, Ibn (1967). (transl.) Rosenthal, F., *The Muqaddimah: An Introduction to History*, 3 vols., Princeton.
Kraemer, J. (1986a). *Humanism in the Renaissance of Islam: The Cultural Revival During the Buyid Age*, Leiden.
— (1986b). *Philosophy in the Renaissance of Islam: Abū Sulaymān al-Sijistānī and His Circle*, Leiden.
Krawulsky, D. (1971). (transl. and ed.) *Briefe und Reden des Abū Hāmid Muḥammad al-Ġazzālī*, Freiburg im Breisgau.
Kühnel, E. (1956). 'Die Kunst Persiens unter den Buyiden', *ZDMG* 106: 78-92.
Kunitzsch, P. 'The Transmission of Hindu-Arabic Numerals Reconsidered', in Hogendijk J. and Sabra A. (eds.), *The Enterprise of Science in Islam: New Perspectives*, Cambridge MA and London.
Lambton, A. K. S. (1973). 'Aspects of Saljuq-Ghuzz Settlement in Persia', in Richards, D. S. (ed.), *Islamic Civilization, 950-1150*, Oxford.
Lang, D. M. (1966). *The Balavariani: A Buddhist Tale from the Christian East*, London.
Lazard, G. (1964). *Les premiers poètes persans (IXe–Xe siècles): fragments rassemblés, édités et traduits*, Tehran and Paris.
— (1971). 'Pahlavi, pârsi, dari: les langues de l'Iran d'après Ibn al-Muqaffa' ', in Bosworth, C. E. (ed.), *Iran and Islam: In Memory of the Late Vladimir Minorsky*, Edinburgh: 361-391.
— (1975). 'The Rise of the New Persian Language', in Frye, R. N. (ed.), *CHIr* 4, Cambridge.
Madelung, W. (1967). 'Abū Isḥāq al-Ṣābī on the Alids of Ṭabaristān and Gīlān', *JNES* 26: 17-57.

— (1975). 'The Minor Dynasties of Northern Iran', in Frye, R. N. (ed.), *CHIr* 4, Cambridge.
— (1969). 'The Assumption of the Title Shāhānshāh by the Būyids and 'The Reign of the Daylam (*Dawlat al-Daylam*)' ', *JNES* 28: 84-108, 169-183.
— (1982). 'Āl-e Bāvand', *EncIr* I: 749-752.
Mahdi, M. *et al.*, (1987). 'Avicenna', *EncIr* III: 66-110.
Marshak, B. (2002). *Legends, Tales, and Fables in the Art of Sogdiana*, SOAS Biennial Ehsan Yarshater Lecture Series 1, New York.
Martin, A. (1984). *Averroès: Grand commentaire de la Métaphysique d'Aristote ... Lambda*, Bibliothèque de la Faculté de philosophie et lettres de l'Université de Liège 234, Paris.
Massignon, L. (1992). 'Nawbakht', *EI*[2] VII: 1043-1044.
Ma'shar, Abu (2000). (transl. and ed.) Yamamoto, K. and Burnett, C., *On Historical Astrology: The Book of Religions and Dynasties (On the Great Conjunctions)*, 2 vols., Leiden, Boston and Köln.
Maysari (1987). (ed.) Zanjani, B., *Dāneshnāme*, Tehran.
Micheau, F. (1994). ' 'Alī ibn al-'Abbās al-Mağūsī et son milieu', in Burnett, C. and Jacquart, D. (eds.), *Constantine the African and 'Alī ibn al-'Abbās al-Mağūsī: The* Pantegni *and Related Texts*, Leiden.
Meister, M. W. (1970). 'The Pearl Roundel in Chinese Textiles', *AO* VIII: 255-267.
Melikian-Chirvani, A. S. (1974). ' L'évocation littéraire du bouddhisme dans l'Iran musulman', *Le monde iranien et l'Islam: sociétés et cultures* II: 1-72.
— (1975). 'Recherches sur l'architecture de l'Iran bouddhique I: Essai sur les origins et le symbolisme du *stupa* iranien', *Le monde iranien et l'Islam: sociétés et cultures* III: 1-61.
Minorsky, V. (1932). *La domination des Daïlamites*, Paris. (Reprinted in *Iranica: Twenty Articles* [*Bīst maqāla-yi Mīnūrskī*], Tehran 1964, 12-30.)
— (1937). *Ḥudūd al-'Ālam: the Regions of the World, a Persian Geography 372 A.H.-982 A.D.*, London.
— (1938). 'Geographical Factors in Persian Art,' *BSO[A]S* IX: 621-652. (Reprinted in *Iranica: Twenty Articles* [*Bīst maqāla-yi Mīnūrskī*], Tehran, 1964: 38-63.)
— (1953). *Studies in Caucasian History*, London.
— (1958). *A History of Sharvān and Darband in the 10th-11th centuries*, Cambridge.
— (1964). *Iranica: Twenty Articles* [*Bīst maqāla-yi Mīnūrskī*], Tehran.
Morony, M. G. (1984). *Iraq after the Muslim Conquest*, Princeton.
Mottahedeh, R. (1976). 'The Shu'ûbiyyah Controversy and the Social History of Early Islamic Iran', *IJMES* 7: 161-182.
Musallam, B. (1987). 'Avicenna x: Biology and Medicine', *EncIr* III: 94-99.
Nikonorov, V. P. (2004). (ed.) *Tsentral'naya Aziya ot Akhemenidov do Timuridov*, St. Petersburg.

Oddy, W. A. (1991). 'Arab Imagery on Early Islamic Coins in Syria and Palestine: Evidence for Falconry', *Numismatic Circular* 151: 59-66.

Pierce, H. and Tyler, R. (1936). 'The Prague Rider-Silk and the Persian-Byzantine Problem', *The Burlington Magazine* LXV: 213-220.

Pingree, D. *et al.*, (1987). 'Astrology and Astronomy in Iran', *EncIr* II: 858-871.

Planhol, X. de (1993). *Les nations du Prophète: Manuel geographique de politique musulmane,* Paris.

Pormann, P. and Savage-Smith, E. (2007). *Medieval Islamic Medicine*, Edinburgh.

Pourshariati, P. (1998). 'Local Histories of Khorasan and the Patterns of Early Settlements', *StIr* 27: 41-81.

— (2008). *Decline and Fall of the Sasanian Empire: The Sasanian-Parthian Confederacy and the Arab Conquest of Iran*, London and New York.

Rashed, R. (1994). (transl.) Armstrong, A., *The Development of Arabic Mathematics: Between Arithmetic and Algebra*, Dordrecht. (Rev. 1984 ed.)

al-Razi (1848). (transl.) Greenhill, W., *A Treatise on the Small-Pox and Measles by Abú Becr Mohammed ibn Zacaríyá ar-Rází (Commonly Called Rhazes),* London.

Richter-Bernburg, L. (1974). 'Linguistic Shu'ūbiyya and Early Neo-Persian Prose,' *JAOS* 94: 54-64.

— (1978). *Persian Medical Manuscripts at the University of California, Los Angeles: A Descriptive Catalogue*, Humana Civilitas 4, Malibu.

— (1980). 'Amīr-Malik-Shāhānshāh: 'Aḍud ad-Daula's Titulature Re-examined' *Iran* 18: 83-102.

— (1994). 'Abu Bakr Muhammad al-Razi's (Rhazes) Medical Works', *Medicina nei Secoli: arte e scienza* 6: 377-392.

— (1998). 'On the Diffusion of Medical Knowledge in Persian Court Culture during the fourth and fifth Centuries A.H.,' in Vesel, Ž. *et al.*, (eds.), *La science dans le monde iranien à l'époque islamique*, Bibliothèque Iranienne 50 (IFRI), Téhéran.

— (1999). 'Iran's Contribution to Medicine and Veterinary Science in Islam AH 100-900/AD 700-1500,' in Greppin J. *et al.*, (eds.), *The Diffusion of Greco-Roman Medicine into the Middle East and the Caucasus*, Delmar.

— (2000). 'Medicine, Pharmacology and Veterinary Science in Islamic Eastern Iran and Central Asia,' in Bosworth, C. E. and Asimov, M. S. (eds.), *History of Civilizations of Central Asia,* IV*: The Age of Achievement: A.D. 750 to the End of the Fifteenth Century. Part Two: The Achievements*, Paris.

— (2005). 'Al-Razi [sic]', in Cooperson, M. and Toorawa, S. (eds.), *Arabic Literary Culture: 500-925*, Detroit.

— (2008). 'Abū Bakr al-Rāzī and al-Fārābī on Medicine and Authority', in Adamson, P. (ed.), *In the Age of al-Fārābī: Arabic Philosophy in the Fourth/Tenth Century*, Warburg Institute Colloquia 12, London and Turin.

Riet, S. van (1972). (ed.) *Avicenna Latinus: Liber de Anima*, I-II-III, Leiden.

Rostovtzeff, M. I. (1943). 'The Parthian Shot', *AJA* 47: 174-187.

Roxburgh, D. (2005). *The Persian Album, 1400-1600: From Dispersal to Collection*, New Haven.
Russell, J. R. (1983). 'The Tale of the Bronze City in Armenian', in Samuelian, T. and Stone, M. (eds.), *Medieval Armenian Culture*, University of Pennsylvania Armenian Texts and Studies 6, Chico: 250-261. (Reprinted in Russell 2004, 9-20).
— (1987). *Yovhannēs T'lkuranc'i and the Mediaeval Armenian Lyric Tradition*, University of Pennsylvania Armenian Texts and Studies 7, Atlanta, GA.
— (1997). 'Zoroastrianism and the Northern Qi Panels', *Zoroastrian Studies*, Bombay. (Reprinted in Russell 2004, 1445-1450).
— (2001). 'The Scepter of Tiridates', *Le Muséon* 114, 1-2: 187-215. (Reprinted in Russell 2004, 1135-1163).
— (2004). *Armenian and Iranian Studies*, Harvard Armenian Texts and Studies 9, Cambridge, MA.
— (2005). 'Solov'i, solov'i', *St. Nersess Theological Review* 10 (2005): 77-139.
— (forthcoming). 'The Rime of the Book of the Dove (*Stikh o Golubinoi knige*): From Zoroastrian Cosmology and Armenian Heresiology to the Russian Novel'.
Sadighi, G. H. (1938). *Les mouvements religieux iranien au IIe et IIIe siècle de l'hégire*, Paris.
al-Sahmi, H. (1950). *Tārīkh Jurjān*, Hyderabad.
Saliba, G. (1992). 'The Role of the Astrologer in Medieval Islamic Society', *BEO* 44: 45-67.
Sarris, P. (2004). 'Rehabilitating the Great Estate', in Bowden, W. *et al.*, *Recent Research on the Late Antique Countryside*, Leiden: 55-71.
— (2006). *Economy and Society in the Age of Justinian*, Cambridge.
Sezgin, F. (1970). *GAS* III, *Mediziri-Pharmazie-Zoolgie-Tierheilkunde bis ca. 430 H.* Leiden.
— (1974). *GAS* V, *Mathematik bis ca. 430 H.* Leiden.
— (1978). *GAS* VI, *Astronomie bis ca. 430 H.* Leiden.
— (1979). *GAS* VII, *Astrologie-Meteorologie und Vermandles bis ca. 430 H.* Leiden.
Shaban, M. A. (1970). *The 'Abbāsid Revolution*, Cambridge.
Shahbazi, A. S. (1989). 'Bahrām. vii. Bahram VI Čōbīn', *EncIr* III: 519-522.
Shalem, A. (2004). 'Bahram Gur Woven with Gold: A Silk Fragment in the Diocesan Museum of St. Afra in Augsburg and the Modes of Rendition of a Popular Theme', in Hillenbrand, R. (ed.), *Shahnama: the Visual Language of the Persian Book of Kings*, Aldershot: 117-127.
Shaw, S. and Polk, W. (1962) (eds.). *Studies on the Civilization of Islam*, Boston.
Silverstein, A. (2007). *Postal Systems in the Pre-modern Islamic World*, Cambridge.
Simonyan, H. (1975). *Hay mijnadaryan kafaner* (*X-XVI dd.*), Erevan.

— (1989). *Patmut'iwn Ałek'sandri Makedonac'woy*, Erevan.
Siroux, M. (1947). 'La mosquée djum'a de Yezd-i-Khast', *BIFO* XLIV: 101-118.
Slezkine, Y. (2004). *The Jewish Century*, Princeton.
Smith, M. B. (1940). 'Three Monuments at Yazd-i Khwast', *AI* VII: 104-106.
Soucek, P. (1974). 'Farhad and Taq-i Bustan: The Growth of a Legend', in Chelkowski, P. J. (ed.), *Studies in Art and Literature of the Near East in Honor of Richard Ettinghausen*, New York and Salt Lake City: 27-52.
Sourdel, D. (1959-60). *Le vizirat 'abbāside de 749 à 936 (132 à 324 de l'hégire)*, 2 vols., Damascus.
Spengler, O. (1937). *The Decline of the West,* New York.
Sprengling, M. (1939). 'From Persian to Arabic Part I', *AJSLL* 56: 175-224, 325-336.
— (1940). 'From Persian to Arabic Part II', *AJSLL* 57: 302-305.
Spuler, F. (1952). *Iran in früh-islamischer Zeit: Politik, Kultur, Verwaltung und öffentliches Leben zwischen der arabischen und der seldschukischen Eroberung 633 bis 1055*, Wiesbaden.
Srpayan, A. (1983). *Patmut'iwn vasn mankann ew ałj kann, Patmut'iwn yałags P'ahlul t'agaworin*, Erevan.
Stern, S. M. (1971). 'Ya'qūb the Coppersmith and Persian National Sentiment', in Bosworth, C. E. (ed.), *Iran and Islam: In Memory of the Late Vladimir Minorsky*, Edinburgh: 535-555.
al-Tabari (1869). (transl.) Zotenberg, H., *Chronique de Tabari, sur la version persane d'Abou-Ali Mohammed Bel'ami*, [vol.] I, Paris.
— (1999). (transl.) Bosworth, C. E., *The History of al-Tabari: the Sasanids, the Byzantines, the Lakhmids, and Yemen*, Albany.
Tha'ālibī (1956-58). (ed.) 'Abd al- Hamid, M. M., *Yatīmat al-dahr wa-mahāsin ahl al-'asr*, Cairo.
— (1968). (transl.) Bosworth, C. E., *The Book of Curious and Entertaining Information*, Edinburgh.
Toomer, G. (1973). , 'al-Khwārizmī', in Gillispie, C. (ed.), *DSB* VII: 358-365.
Tor, D. (2007). *Violent Order: Religious Warfare, Chivalry and the 'Ayyār Phenomenon in the Medieval Islamic World*, Würzburg.
Toynbee, A. J. (1961). *A Study of History,* 12 vols., Oxford.
Treadwell, L. (2001). *Buyid Coinage: A Die Corpus (322-445 A.H.)*, Oxford.
— (2003). 'Shāhānshāh and al-Malik al-Mu'ayyad: The Legitimation of Power in Sāmānid and Būyid Iran,' in Daftary, F. and Meri, J. (eds.), *Culture and Memory in Medieval Islam: Essays in Honour of Wilfred Madelung*, London and New York.
Utas, Bo. (2006). 'A Multi-ethnic Origin of New Persian?', in Johanson, Lars and Bulut, Christine (eds.), *Turkic-Iranian Contact Areas: Historical and Linguistic Aspects,* Turcologica 62, Wiesbaden.
Vernet, J. (1978). 'al-Khwārazmī, Abū Dja'far Muḥammad b.Mūsā', *EI*[2] IV: 1070-1071.

Vico, G. (1948). (transl.) Bergin, T. G. and Fisch, M. H., *The New Science*, Ithaca.
Volbach, W. F. (1969). (transl.) Gabriel, Y., *Early Decorative Textiles*, Feltham.
Walker, J. (1941). *A Catalogue of the Arab-Sussanian Coins in the British Museum (Umaiyad Governors in the East, Arab-Ephthalites, 'Abbasid Governors in Tabaristan and Bukhara)*, London.
Wang, E. (2005). *Shaping the Lotus Sutra: Buddhist Visual Culture in Medieval China*, Seattle.
Watson, B. (1993). (transl.) *The Lotus Sutra*, New York.
Weisser, U. (1987). 'Avicenna xiii: The Influence of Avicenna on Medical Studies in the West', *EncIr* III: 107-110.
Wellhausen, J. (1927). *The Arab Kingdom and Its Fall*, Calcutta.
Wiedemann, E. (1912). 'Beiträge zur Geschichte der Naturwissenschaften. XXVII', *Sitzungsberichte der Physikalisch-Medizinischen Sozietät in Erlangen* 44: 1-40.
Wittfogel, K. (1957). *Oriental Despotism: A Comparative Study of Total Power*, New Haven and London.
al-Ya'qubi (1937). (transl.) Wiet, G., *Kitāb al-Buldān* [*Les pays*], Cairo.
Yarshater, E. (1983). (ed.) *CHIr* 3(2), *The Seleucid, Parthian and Sasanian Periods*, Cambridge.
Zarrinkub, 'Abd al-Husain. (1975). 'The Arab Conquest of Iran and Its Aftermath', in Frye, R. N. (ed.), *CHIr* 4, Cambridge.
Zonta, M. (2006). 'The Jewish Mediation in the Transmission of Arabo-Islamic Science and Philosophy to the Latin Middle Ages. Historical Overview and Perspectives of Research', in Speer, A. and Wegener, L. (eds.), *Wissen über Grenzen: Arabisches Wissen und lateinisches Mittelalter*, Berlin and New York.